# T I B E T

# Preface

I, the old man, cheerfully sing this song
Of joy and pleasure, that will bring
Auspicious luck and fortune.

The high crystal peak that mirrors the first beams
Of sunlight in the morning is the crown,
Beautified by white hanging clouds.

Clinging to the lower Mount
Is perpetual mist and fog;
All day long the drizzle gently falls,
While rainbows brightly shine.
Here autumn flowers bloom
In different colors,
And thrive potent herbs
In great varieties.
This is the paradise of cattle,
This homeland of animals!
This is the Snow Mountain
The gods talk most about,
This is where I often meditate.

*From The Hundred Thousand Songs of Milarepa, translated by
Garma C C Chang*

*(Previous Page)*
On a rock at Drepung Monastery is
the image of Khedrub Jey
(1385–1438), one of the two chief
disciples of Tsong Khapa, founder
of the Gelugpa Order. Khedrub Jey
served as an early abbot of Ganden
Monastery.

*(Right)*
Carved on a yak's skull is the
mantra Om Mani Padme Hum
(O precious jewel in the lotus). It
rests on a mound by the shore of
sacred Lake Namtso. On the far
side of the lake is the Nyenchen
Thanglha Range.

A nomad camp near Mount Kailash in western Tibet. Even during the most temperate time of year little grass grows at this altitude.

A nomad family's tent a week before the Lhabab Duchen Festival. The festival takes place every year on the 22nd day of the ninth lunar month (early November) and commemorates the Buddha's legendary descent from Heaven where he had been to visit his sainted mother. Pilgrims circumambulate the stupa on a nearby hill.

Nomads gather their horses after
taking part in the Lhabab Duchen
Festival.

*(Above)*
An exquisite 15th-century wall painting of Archetypal Buddhas
in father-mother union, known as yab-yum in Tibetan, at the
Great Stupa in Gyantse. The male deity is holding a dorje
(thunderbolt scepter) in his right hand which is placed at the
center of a lotus. The dorje and lotus symbolize great bliss and
wisdom, as well as the male and female sexual organs.
*(Previous pages)*
A distant view of the wilderness as seen from the ruins of
Tsaparang, one-time capital of the 10th-century
Guge Kingdom in West Tibet.

# TIBET

## KAZUYOSHI NOMACHI

Introduction by Robert A. F. Thurman

Foreword by the 14th Dalai Lama

SHAMBHALA
*Boston*
1997

Published by Shambhala Publications, Inc.
Horticultural Hall
300 Massachusetts Avenue
Boston, Massachusetts 02115
http://www.shambhala.com

9 8 7 6 5 4 3 2 1

First Shambhala Edition

Printed in Hong Kong

Distributed in the United States by Random House, Inc.,
and in Canada by Random House of Canada Ltd

Design: Yuji Nakajo, Philip Choi

Map illustration: Shoichi Masuda

ISBN 1-57062-256-6
LC 97–3533

# Contents

PREFACE *2*

FOREWORD BY THE 14ᵀᴴ DALAI LAMA *16*

INTRODUCTION *17*

MAP OF TIBET *21*

MOUNT KAILASH *22*

THE COSMIC AXIS: A PERSONAL PRILGRIMAGE *44*

TIBET: MOUNTAINS AND PLATEAU *48*

LIVING WITH THE YAKS *94*

DAYS OF TIBETAN BUDDHISM *97*

PURE LAND OF THE BUTTER LAMPS *144*

REMAINS OF THE GUGE KINGDOM *148*

SHATTERED LAND OF THE BUDDHA *172*

THE KALACHAKRA INITIATION *176*

INTERVIEW WITH THE 14ᵀᴴ DALAI LAMA *188*

MODERN TIBET *192*

CHRONOLOGY OF TIBETAN HISTORY *195*

AFTERWORD *197*

ACKNOWLEDGEMENTS *198*

# Foreword by His Holiness the 14th Dalai Lama

The land of Tibet consists of a huge plateau isolated from neighbouring countries by its altitude and encircling mountain ranges. Over much of the country's history the authorities have pursued a policy of isolation, deliberately keeping contacts with the outside world to a minimum. This policy may have served Tibet well to begin with, but it became one of the reasons we lost our country. This physical and political isolation led to an air of mystery surrounding the Tibetan people, their culture and way of life. Consequently, the Chinese, once they occupied our country, have been able to propagate distorted images of the Land of the Snows.

Although Tibet's climate is severe, the land consists of unspoilt, wide-open spaces under a deep blue sky. Before the Chinese occupation we were not rich, but we had all we needed and our people never went hungry. The sense of freedom and contentment that we enjoyed, combined with the strength we drew from our Buddhist faith, meant that we truly lived in peace.

Sadly, all this came to an end in 1950 when the People's Liberation Army invaded Tibet. At that time I was just a 15-year-old monk pursuing my studies. The Tibetan National Assembly, faced with this unprecedented occupation, called upon me to head the nation.

The situation steadily worsened and faced with an overwhelming military power, there was only one course open to me to avoid any violent confrontation. To challenge the Chinese militarily would have been suicidal. I determined then that Tibetan freedom could only be regained by non-violence. Eventually, tension in the capital, Lhasa, became so great that in March 1959 I had to flee my homeland and seek asylum in India. I was followed by about 100,000 of my fellow-countrymen who escaped to India and other neighbouring countries.

In those early days we did not imagine that 35 years later we would still be living in exile. Fortunately, due to the kindness and support of many friends, particularly the government and people of India, the Tibetans in exile have not only resettled well but also thrived. We have extremely successful settlement colonies and schools for our children. Many people, including journalists, have remarked that the Tibetan life in exile is a refugee success story. Many of our monasteries and nunneries have been re-established and their particular courses of training revived. Besides these, new institutions have been founded to preserve and develop such traditions as medicine, arts and crafts, performing arts and literary skills.

We are proud that we have been able to preserve in exile the Tibetan national identity and culture, which is deeply influenced by the Buddhist teachings of love, compassion, kindness, tolerance and the theory that all things are relative. The practice of these concepts, I believe, has proved to be very helpful when we have faced tragedy. The interest shown by the world in the plight of the Tibetan people and the spirituality of Tibetan culture has also been very encouraging.

Regarding the future of Tibet, I am optimistic. Changes are taking place in China. It is only a matter of time before Tibet and China enjoy freedom and democracy. My dream is for Tibet to be genuinely democratic and eventually fully demilitarised. The whole of Tibet should become a sanctuary, a zone of peace and non-violence. In this way Tibet could again serve as a peaceful buffer between the two Asian giants, India and China. Visitors from all over the world will then be welcomed in Tibet to enjoy and share our experience of peace and harmony. I believe that the transformation of Tibet into a zone of peace could serve, like Costa Rica, as a model for contributing towards maintaining peace in the Asian region and the world at large.

Meanwhile, it is most important that people the world over are made aware of what Tibet once was, and what has happened there over these last 40 years of hostile and ruthless Chinese occupation. The Tibetan issue not only remains alive, but goes from strength to strength, as more and more people come to understand the justice of our struggle for freedom and our earnest desire to live in peace. Everything that helps us achieve this is valuable. I therefore welcome this pictorial book on Tibet by Kazuyoshi Nomachi and hope it will further enhance the outside world's appreciation of my country and its people.

28th August, 1993

# Introduction

The Tibetans are not a "primitive," "medieval," "feudal," "backward," or even "non-literate" people. Their unique national character is much more complex. Their recorded history dates back at least some 2300 years, to the time of the Macedonian Greek empire in the west, the Mauryan empire in India, and the late Chou empire in China. During Tibet's first nine centuries, it was ruled by a militaristic conquest dynasty. Like other ancient civilizations, its religious system was animistic, run by a priesthood expert in divination, sorcery, and sacrifice. Its myth centered on a royal family descended from the heavens on a mountaintop, later scions being entombed in huge burial mounds, like Egyptian Pharaohs.

This early dynasty was based in the Yarlung Valley, near a major river on the high plateau, the Brahmaputra. It gradually united the lords of neighboring kingdoms in a feudal, military network. The tribes of the plateau were already connected by three common bonds; a unique territory, related languages, and a common religious tendency. They inhabited the almost one-million-square-mile high plateau, with an average altitude of over 14,000 feet. Their languages belonged to the Tibeto-Burman language family, distinct from the Indic, Turkic, Mongolian, and Sinitic language families of the surrounding lowlands. Religiously, all tended to deify elements of nature, especially mountains and sky, and shared a fondness for rituals of sacrifice and divination, propitiating a diverse pantheon of underworld, landscape, and celestial deities. Their high-altitude cultures were distinguished from lowland ones by the intensity of their spiritual orientation. Lifespans at high altitude are short, death is an immediate presence, and the spectacular mountain landscape is conducive to contemplation. Like most shamanisms, ancient Tibetan spirituality sought mundane success—victory, health, wealth, and progeny.

This militaristic culture was successful for many centuries. Rivals from surrounding lowlands could not intrude for long on the high plateau. The Tibetans' struggles with their natural environment and with each other strengthened them. By the sixth century CE they had become an empire with a fearsome reputation.

At the start of the Yarlung dynasty, Buddhism was already two hundred years old in India, originated by Shakyamuni Buddha around 500 BCE. It was not based on a revelation received from a deity, as the Buddha rejected belief in an omnipotent world Creator. He did not even consider faith an end in itself, though he accepted reasonable beliefs as practically useful. He encouraged people to question authority, use their reason and not accept irrational traditions. He was called a "Buddha," an "Awakened" or "Enlightened" person, because he claimed to have gained a perfect understanding of the nature and structure of reality. Having reached such full understanding himself, he felt that other humans would also be able to achieve it. He dedicated the next forty-five years to teaching all kinds of people; and history records that large numbers did reach high levels of realization. They formed a movement that gradually spread over the Indian subcontinent and most of Asia.

The Buddha used the Sanskrit word "Dharma" to designate his Truth or Teaching. "Dharma" came from the verb root /dhr, "to hold", and had a range of meanings. It could mean "phenomenon," "custom," "duty," or "law"—any held pattern. It could also mean "religion," as a held pattern of belief and ritual. But the core of the Buddha's discovery was the essential reality of freedom—that underlying the lived reality of existence is the immediacy of total freedom, especially freedom from suffering, bondage, and ignorance. He saw that this essential freedom can be realized by the human mind as its own deepest condition, which realization makes freedom prevail over the habitual suffering in personal experience. The realized individual is thenceforth held apart from suffering; not held in anything, but held out of binding patterns; hence the new range of meanings of "Dharma". After Buddha, Dharma came to mean the "Teaching," the "Path" of practice of the Teaching, the "Virtue" of that practice, the "Reality" or "Truth" taught in that Teaching, and the "Freedom" of that Reality or Truth, that is, Nirvana itself.

The Buddha founded an educational movement that developed historically on three levels: the social, the religious, and the philosophical or scientific. During his time there were many views of the nature of life, ranging from spiritualistic soul theories to a strikingly modern materialism. He rejected all absolute soul theories, postulations of a rigidly fixed identity or static personal essence. He taught that the cognitive and emotional habit of assuming a fixed subjectivity or identity was a key obstacle to a good life. But he did not reject the relative presence of a living self, the continuity of the changeable, fluid soul from life to life. He upheld the rebirth of the relative self and rejected the contemporary nihilism that reduced the relative soul or self to a random epiphenomenon of matter. He taught the relative self's reality, responsibility, and evolutionary potential.

His teaching of the universal relativity of the self opened up a popular vision of the vast interconnectedness of the individual with the boundless forms of life. This vision inspired the normal Buddhist determination to consciously evolve toward individual fulfillment and to transform the whole world into a positive environment. The Mahayana scriptures teach that a Buddha is a cosmic being whose state is described as consisting of Three Bodies. A Buddha's perfect wisdom becomes a Truth Body, a Body which is the experience of the whole universe as one with his or her own being. A Buddha's perfect compassion becomes a Form Body, which has two aspects; a Beatific Body, which is the ethereal body of bliss energy that enjoys the universal freedom of oneness with the ultimate, and an Emanation Body which is irrepressibly creative of emanated embodiments that interact liberatively with all suffering beings. The Three Bodies, Truth, Beatific, and Emanation, provide a key framework for understanding the Tibetan sense of the inconceivable reality and presence of enlightened beings.

In the early seventh century, an emperor named Songtsen Gambo brought the empire to its natural limits. He then began to transform the civilization from feudal militarism to something more peaceful and spiritual. He investigated the major civilizations of Outer Asia, and saw that Mahayana Buddhism provided the cultural backbone of the post-Gupta dynasties of India, the silk route city states of Central Asia, and the T'ang dynasty of China. He sent a team of scholars to India to learn Sanskrit, create a written language for Tibetan and translate the vast Buddhist literature. He married nine queens from surrounding countries, including Nepal and T'ang China, asking each to bring Buddhist artifacts and texts with her to Tibet. He built a geomantic system of imperial temples, centered on the Jokhang and Ramoche cathedrals around which he built in his new capital at Lhasa.

During the following centuries, his successors continued his work of cultural transformation, sponsoring translations, holding research conferences, building institutions and educating their subjects. This process reached a high point during the 790's. The Emperor Trisong Detsen, with the help of the Indian adept Padma Sambhava and the Indian Buddhist abbot Shantirakshita, built the first monastic university at Samye. The Indian Buddhist university curriculum was transplanted, and a fifty-year process of collecting all the useful knowledge then available in Asia was begun. Mathematics, poetry, medicine, the art of government, art and architecture—all these branches of learning were cultivated, not only Buddhist philosophy and psychology. Scholars were invited from all cultures, and Tibetans compared their sciences in the quest for the best understanding of man and nature.

During the 830's, hundreds of scholars spent a decade comparing the medical systems of India, China, Persia, and Mongolia, creating a Tibetan medical system that integrated the best available psychology, anatomy, neurology, surgery, botany, chemistry, and nutrition with the Buddhist spiritual technology.

In the ninth century, a period of confusion ensued, due to organized resistance to the imposition of Buddhist ethics and practices upon a militaristic society. There was an anti-Buddhist persecution, and a series of assassinations ended with the fragmentation of the nation. Soon, however, Buddhist insights and institutions re-emerged, now rooted among the people, with sponsorship from regional rulers. From the tenth to the thirteenth centuries Tibetans turned their interests increasingly toward Buddhist education; monasteries were built all over the country. The vast work of translation was completed and a voluminous indigenous literature was developed. No new dynasty emerged to control the whole country, militarism being unable to return due to the power of Buddhism and its morality of nonviolence. Local noble families began to share their social and political power with the rapidly developing monastic institutions.

During the 13th century, the Mongolian empire unified most of Eurasia, and Tibet formally submitted to Mongol rule. The land was divided into thirteen main administrative regions, each run by a local combination of a noble family and a monastic hierarchy. The Sakyapa Order was put in charge over all by Khubilai Khan. In the middle of the 14th century, the Mongol empire fell apart, a Tibetan secular dynasty arose, and a spiritual renaissance was ushered in by the life work of Lama Jey Tsong Khapa. This era of national dedication to the practice of Buddhism as the main aim of life was sealed by his founding the Great Prayer (Monlam Chenmo) Festival in Lhasa in 1409, to celebrate the nation's dawning awareness of the imminent presence of the Buddha. Thius began the tradition for the whole nation to come together for two weeks of prayer every lunar new year, all ordinary business suspended. This festival was a core event in Lhasa from 1409 until 1959.

During the 15th and 16th centuries, the renaissance initiated by Tsong Khapa transformed the spiritual, social, and physical landscape of Tibet. In region after region, monastery building intensified as numerous men and women became determined to dedicate their "precious human lives endowed with freedom and opportunity" to fulfill their evolution and attain enlightenment. The social climate became more peaceful, as fewer individuals were available for the armies of the remaining local warlords. One of Tsong Khapa's disciples, Gendun Drubpa, led the new Gelukpa Order during a long and creative life of inspiring teaching, writing, and building. A few years after his death in 1474, a beautiful young boy claimed to be Gendun Grubpa reborn. After many tests he was accepted as the actual reincarnation of the great master, and was educated for leadership as the Lama Gendun Gyatso. His subsequent reincarnation, Sonam Gyatso, led the Order in the 16th century. During a visit to Mongolia in 1573, he was named "Dalai Lama" ("Oceanic Master") by the Mongolian King Altan Khan. Counting his two predecessors, Sonam Gyatso became known as His Holiness the Third Dalai Lama.

During his time and that of his successor the Tibetan nobles, still feudal warlords, began to feel threatened by the steady wave of spiritual renaissance, popular dedication to enlightenment, education, and money- and time-consuming monastery-building. A period of turbulence ensued around the turn of the 17th century, with the fate of the country in the balance. Would the secular forces of the remaining aristocratic warlords prevail, curtailing the ascendancy of the monastery-centered lifestyle, in parallel with what was happening at the time in northern Europe, China, and Japan? Or would the warlords give up their ways of violence, lay down their arms, and once and for all embrace the path of spiritual evolution?

In 1642, one thousand years after the building of the Jokhang cathedral, the Fifth Dalai Lama (1617-1682) was crowned king of Tibet, founding the Ganden Palace Victory Government. The "Great Fifth" created a unique form of monastic government, well suited to Tibet's special society. It was almost completely demilitarized, acknowledging the priority given to nonviolence and the centrality of the monastic institutions. The warlords were neutralized, retaining the income from parts of their hereditary estates only as salary for service to the government. Their private armies were disbanded, and they lost their feudal power of life and death over their peasants, who had been like the serfs of Russia and Europe.

After the Dalai Lama's trip to China in 1651, Tibetan independence was guaranteed by the new pan-Asian emperors of the era, the Manchus, a Tungusic people from the forests north of Korea, who had conquered northern China in 1644. The Manchus recognized the Dalai Lama's secular authority over Tibet and his spiritual authority over the world as they knew it. The Dalai Lama recognized the Manchus as legitimate rulers of Manchuria and China and as international protectors of the Buddhist Dharma. The Dalai Lama agreed to encourage the Mongols to practice Buddhism, and the Manchus agreed to protect the peace for the demilitarized Buddhist societies.

The Tibetan pacification of the Mongols, the demilitarization of that most militarily powerful society, is one of the remarkable social transformations in history, as amazing as Tibet's transformation over the previous millennium and India's transformation during the twelve hundred years previous. Due to its demilitarization after the 17th century, Tibetan society is no longer properly called "feudal," a term desciibing a pre-modern but militaristic organization of society.

During the three centuries of Tibet's modern period (1642-1959), the national priority was on monastic education, literary and philosophical creativity, the practice of meditation, the development of the ritual and festival arts and so forth. Spiritual adepts were honored as the highest level of Tibetan society, considered to have become perfected Buddhas through their practice of the spiritual technologies of the Unexcelled Yoga Tantras. They voyaged to the furthest reaches of the inner frontiers of consciousness itself, in all its transformations in life and beyond death. They developed the ability consciously to pass through the dissolution process, to detach from the gross physical body and use a "magic" or "virtual" body to travel to other universes. They were believed to have mastered the death, between, and rebirth processes, and to choose continuously, life after life, to return to Tibet out of compassion to lead the Tibetans in their spiritual national life and to benefit all sentient beings. These adepts were the Dalai Lamas and the several thousand other reincarnate Lamas.

Modern Tibetan civilization was unique on the planet, therefore not yet recognized. The stereotype of "backward" and "primitive" comes from the Tibetan choice to retain an intermediate level of material technology, putting their national effort into spiritual attainment. I call the unique psychological character complex of modern Tibetans "inner modernity."

It contrasts with the modern Western psychological character complex, which I call "outer modernity," (usually called simply "modernity" and contrasted with the pre-modern "primitive" or "traditional" character). This modern Western character complex is often described as a complex of traits such as individualism, flexibility of identity, restless reflectiveness, and adherence to rationality. It is connected with a peculiar perception of all things—including psychic or mental things—as ultimately reducible to quantifiable material entities. This is what gives it its "outwardness." The modern Tibetan character complex shares the modern traits of individualism, flexibility of identity, reflectiveness, and rationality. But the Tibetan character is bound up with its peculiar perception, derived from Buddhist civilization, of all things as infused with spiritual value, as interconnected with mental states. This is what gives it its "inwardness."

Thus while Western and Tibetan personalities share the complex of modernity of consciousness, they are diametrically opposed in outlook, one focused outward on matter and the other inward on mind. This difference of personality underlies the difference between the two civilizations. The Western life-purpose is ever greater material productivity, and the Tibetan life-purpose is ever greater spiritual attainment. Spiritual attainment is measured by how deeply one's wisdom can be developed, how broadly one's compassion can exert itself. Tibetans believe that outer reality is interconnected with inner mental development over a beginningless and endless series of lives, so they see no limit to how much the self and the environment can be transformed for the better. An individual can become a Buddha, a being of perfect wisdom and compassion; and the environment can become a perfect Buddha-land, wherein no one suffers pointlessly and all are there for the happiness of all.

Tibetan inwardly directed reason put the material world second on its list of priorities. Its prime concern was the world of inner experience, the waking, gross realm of causality, relativity, sensation, percept and concept, and the subtle realm of image, light, ecstasy, trance, dream, and finally, death and its beyond. The Tibetans considered this inner, subtlemost, experiential realm the important point at which to assert control of all subjective and objective cosmic events. And so the Tibetans set about exploring this inner world, using analytic insight and contemplative concentration to extend their awareness. They used dreams and inner visions to visit lucidly the territories of the unconscious. They used focused dis-identification with coarse subjectivity to gain access to the subtlest level of sentience. And they used an augmented sense of mindfulness and memory to gain access to past life experience, including the dream-like experiences of the between states traversed from death to birth.

In this elegant volume of the beautiful photographs of Kazuyoshi Nomachi, animated by his account of his deep experiences and his instinctive sense of kinship with the Tibetan people, we can see more clearly if we remove the tinted glasses of stereotypes such as "primitive" or "backward," and look for the incredible stark directness, the friendly spirituality and the shining intelligence of the people and for the magical, illuminated quality of the striking landscape within which generations of Tibetans cultivated their hearts and minds.

In spite of too much neglect of its material development, Tibet developed during its modern period into a relatively happy land. Tibetan society was organized to maximize the individual's potential for inner development, economic pressure was mild, and conflict within and warfare without was rare. However, it was still far from a perfected Buddha-land. In modern geopolitical terms, it became highly vulnerable during our century, due to one positive quality and one negative quality. Positively, it was long demilitarized and therefore no match for the mechanized armies of first the British and then the Chinese. Negatively, it had become too isolated from other nations, locking them out as Buddhism disappeared from them. Consequently, the only two nations who did have a little knowledge of Tibet, the British and the Chinese, were able to misrepresent Tibet to the rest of the world to suit their immediate self-interest. When the British wanted to enact trade agreements with the sovereign Tibetan government, they dealt with Tibet as the independent nation that it was. Meanwhile, they let the world at large think of Tibet as under China, to keep the Russians out and to keep the Chinese happy, pleased for the British to retain possession of Hong Kong and its valuable trade opportunities. The Chinese likewise knew very well they did not control Tibet, that Tibetans had no sense of being Chinese, and that no Chinese person had ever had the slightest feeling that any Tibetan was a kind of Chinese. Yet they still pretended to the world that they owned Tibet, that it had always been a part of China. Thus when the Maoist government invaded Tibet in 1950, they told the world they were "liberating" their own country's Tibetan province from foreigners (there were a handful of Chinese and half a dozen Europeans in Tibet at that time).

But since Tibetans considered the Chinese to be foreigners, they resisted being "liberated" to the death. But the Red Army overwhelmed the Buddhist Tibetans, and the Chinese occupation ever since has only endured by brute force. Over a million Tibetans have died unnaturally, and the entire Buddhist culture has been shattered. Not a single Tibetan does not dream and pray to be free and independent of the invaders. Nomachi has intuited this feeling in the Tibetan heart, and he is to be much commended for not shrinking from honestly conveying their sufferings, their feelings, and their undying hope.

In order to transform Tibet into a part of China, the Chinese have attempted to suppress the Tibetan language, Buddhism and the culture based on it, and all vestiges of Tibetan national identity. Such a project is doomed to failure, as the Tibetans simply cannot make themselves into Chinese. The attempt to make Tibetans into Chinese ends up killing off the Tibetans. Fortunately, during this time His Holiness the Fourteenth Dalai Lama has succeeded in maintaining a healthy community in exile, with the patronage of the Government of India.

This wonderful visual monument to the human reality of Tibet can play a vital role in awakening the world to its special value and its horrendous situation. Nomachi's penetrating photographic eye reveals a culture and a people in real danger of extinction. We must hope and insist that the nations of the world, as they learn the truth about Tibet in time, will not allow the genocide of the six million Tibetans to be completed in the opening decade of the twenty-first century.

*Robert A. F. Thurman*
Jey Tsong Khapa Professor of Indo-Tibetan Buddhist Studies
Columbia University in the City of New York

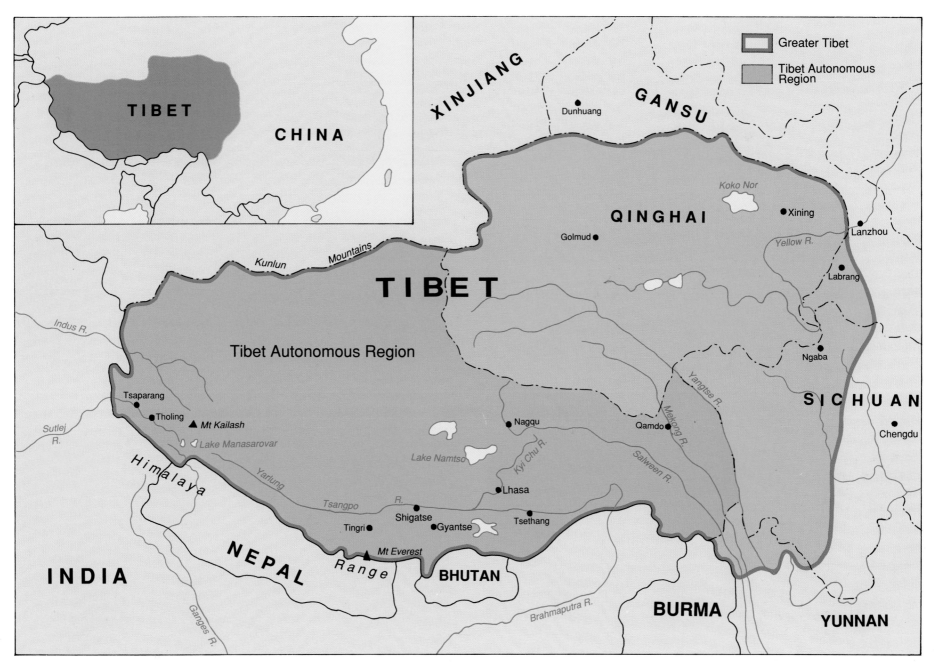

Map showing the political bound-
aries of Tibet, old and new. The
area within the green line encom-
passes "ethnic Tibet," the area recognized by the British as Tibet in
the Simla Treaty of 1914. The
dotted lines show how this area
has been divided up by the
Chinese administration into
Qinghai province (formerly the
Tibetan province of Amdo), the
Tibetan Autonomous Prefectures
of Gansu, Sichuan, and Yunnan
(formerly most of Kham
province), and the Tibet
Autonomous Region (formerly U,
Tsang, and Ngari provinces, less
than half of old Tibet).

# Mount Kailash

In ancient India there was a cosmic theory that at the centre of the universe stood a peak called Mount Sumeru, abode of the gods, around which revolved the sun and moon. It was both a metaphysical and actual center, an axis that connected various planes of existence, including our own human world. And there was an actual mountain on earth that served as this center of the world.

For Hindus that mountain is Kailash, rising far away to the north, among the high ranges of the world's highest plateau. As if to confirm the glory of religious expectation, the geography of the Kailash region is unparalleled. Mount Kailash stands as a beacon on the Roof of the World, isolated in its grandeur, and from its vicinity radiate four of Asia's mightiest rivers. They are the Indus, the Sutlej, the Brahmaputra and the Karnali, the last a major tributary of the holy Ganges. The Indus and Brahmaputra embrace the entire Indian subcontinent like two great arms, one flowing into the Arabian Sea, the other into the Bay of Bengal. The rivers are the very life-blood of the vast zones that they traverse, essential for the well-being of Tibetans and Indians.

Hindus also believe Mount Kailash is the home of Lord Shiva, one of Hinduism's three chief gods; his flowing, matted locks are the source of the great rivers. The mountain is also Shiva's linga, the cosmic phallus, and below it lies Lake Manasarowar, a huge yoni, often symbolized as a lotus, that fulfills the feminine principle of the universe. In Tibetan they are called Khang Rinpoche (Jewel of Snows) and Mapham Tso (Lake Invincible).

Prior to the introduction of Buddhism into Tibet in the seventh century, most Tibetans followed the way of Bon, an ancient religion originating from Iran.

For the followers of Bon, the Bonpo, Kailash was at the heart of the ancient Shangshung Kingdom and stood as their soul-montain, which to this day they call Yungdrung Gutse, the Nine-Storey Swastika Mountain. This is the very place where Bon's legendary founder, Tonpa Shenrab, descended to earth from heaven. The Bonpo faithful consider a pilgrimage to the auspicious Swastika Mountain a high point in life.

West Tibet saw the revival of Buddhism in the 11th century. At this time the charismatic Milarepa, poet-saint and patriarch of the Kagyu sect, lived in the Kailash region and won the area for Buddhism through a famous series of contests of magic with his Bonpo rival.

Milarepa's order flourished, and from the 12th century onwards monasteries, temples and retreats sprang up near the slopes of Mount Kailash and by the shores of Lake Manasarowar. This period marked the arrival of large numbers of pilgrims from all over Tibet. To Buddhist believers, the mountain has always been the abode of the Buddha Demchok (Supreme Bliss), an ecstatic, Tantric manifestation who works with Shiva to ensure the welfare of the universe.

The aim of a pilgrimage to Mount Kailash is to expiate the sins committed in this life, gain religious merit and pray for rebirth as a human being, free from the torments of the lesser and demonic realms. People from both sides of the Himalayas have honoured the mountain for millennia and continue to make it a holy destination, even if it takes a whole lifetime to get there.

It can be said without exaggeration that Kailash is Asia's most sacred mountain.

The north face of Mount Kailash at sunrise. In Tibet, the mountain is known as Khang Rinpoche, 'Precious Jewel of Snows'. The Tibetans consider Kailash to be a manifestation of the Buddha Supreme Bliss Wheel (Chakrasamvara) and the surrounding peaks to be other Buddhas, and they worship the area as a natural mandala. It is said that a solemn wish made here in front of the north face will definitely come true, sooner or later.

Rivers from the Kailash range flow into two lakes. One is the sacred Lake Manasarowar, the other malign Lake Rakshastal, seen here. Mount Kailash stands in the far distance.

*(Above)*
The south face of Mount Kailash covered in ice. Fissures and striations running the length and breadth of Kailash are said to depict the auspicious swastika sign. At the lower right pilgrims gather at Dharchen for the Saga Dawa Festival during the full moon of the fourth lunar month. The festival marks the Buddha's Enlightenment as well as his death and attainment of parinirvana.

*(Right)*
Tibetan pilgrims head for Mount Kailash, a destination denied them by the Chinese until 1982. All 14 temples in the Kailash region were destroyed during the Cultural Revolution.

*(Clockwise from top-left)*

Pilgrims on the circuit around sacred Lake Manasarowar.

These pilgrims spent days sitting in the back of this truck, exposed to the cold wind of the high plateau.

Pilgrims without tents camp in the open with a blanket and eat the same fare every day: tsampa (roasted barley flour), butter tea and dried meat.

A nomad child arrives at Mount Kailash in a basket tied to the back of a yak. The yak's horns have been cut to avoid injuries.

A nomad girl has applied tocha to her face, a cosmetic made from either concentrated buttermilk or roots. It protects the skin from ultraviolet rays and dryness.

*(Above)*
The prayer Om Mani Padme Hum carved on a mani stone. All sacred places in Tibet have piles of such stones that have been offered by devotees.

*(Right)*
A pilgrim circumambulates the stupa at Dharchen, the Kailash pilgrim base. He chants prayers and continuously turns a prayer wheel in his left hand. In western Tibet, a near desert, one frequently comes across men wearing goggles to protect their eyes from dust and ultraviolet rays.

Along the pilgrim route on the western side of Mount Kailash. Buddhists always circle the object of veneration in a clockwise direction.

A man circumnambulates Mount Kailash by performing body-length prostrations. One round of Kailash is about 52 kilometres (32 miles) and takes two weeks to complete in this way. The circuit includes snow-covered mountain paths that rise to 5,636 metres (18,500 feet). Pilgrims come to Kailash to atone for their sins and to ensure they are reborn in the human world, rather than in hell or as hungry ghosts.

*(Left)*
A man takes a short break from his prostrations. Before starting the day's devotions he will have moved his belongings to where he expects to finish at the end of the day. He wears an apron made of leather and mittens made of old tyres.

*(Right)*
Once pilgrims start doing prostrations they cannot take any short cuts or skip any difficult sections of the route, such as icy streams or frozen ground. The greater the suffering the greater the merit gained. Prostrating requires lots of strength, so mostly young men perform such devotions.

*(Previous Pages)*
Some Tibetans believe that the summit of Mount
Kailash is the mythic Mount Sumeru, Abode of
the Gods of the Thirty Three Heaven, while others
believe a ladder at the top reaches other Heavens.
For Hindus, Mount Kailash represents the linga
(phallus) of Lord Shiva and Lake Manasarowar is
the yoni (vulva) of Shakti, the female principle.

*(Above)*
A pilgrim prays at Silwa Tsel, a sacred
spot on the Dolma La Pass. Pilgrims
leave behind clothes, hats, hair and
other objects, and some even shed a
few drops of blood. By doing so they
expiate their sins and deposit proof
that they have been on the holy
Kailash pilgrimage circuit.

The Dolma La Pass, 5,636 metres (18,500 feet) above sea level, is the highest point along the pilgrim route. When people reach it they shout 'So-so-so, Lha Gyalo!' (Victory to the Gods), hoist prayer flags and throw tsampa in the air to ensure that they have good fortune and are protected from evil.

*(Above)*
Pilgrims walk down a rocky slope.
Their clothing suggests they are from
the Dingri region of Central Tibet.

*(Right)*
A family presses on through the sleet.

# The Cosmic Axis: A Personal Pilgrimage

In 1984, in a documentary film shown by the Japan Broadcasting Corporation (NHK), I saw sacred Mount Kailash for the first time. The most enthralling thing was not the mountain itself but the pilgrims converging on it. Many had taken years to reach their destination, some prostrating themselves the entire way, inchworm fashion. One man, a one-legged Hindu from Calcutta, had taken 20 years to reach the Kailash area. In the age of the global village, when cultures are becoming increasingly uniform, the sight of ordinary people with such tremendous faith and a sole purpose in life is astonishing.

Mount Kailash is situated in remote Western Tibet and for much of the 1980s lay within a restricted area. However, in May 1990 I got a chance to go there. I persuaded a television director friend of mine to let me join a team he was taking to the region.

The timing of our visit was auspicious because it coincided with the Saga Dawa festival. According to the Tibetan calendar, the 15th day of the fourth month commemorates the Enlightenment of Shakyamuni Buddha, as well as his birth, death and attainment of nirvana. Also, 1990 was the Year of the Horse and Tibetans believe that a pilgrimage to Mount Kailash during Saga Dawa in this year bestows the greatest merit.

The gathering of pilgrims at the sacred mountain also coincided with the first anniversary of the Tiananmen incident and there was a possibility of demonstrations against the Chinese during the festival.

Our team met in Kathmandu, Nepal, and then moved on to Zhangmu on the Tibetan border. Six Tibetan guides with two Landcruisers and a truck loaded with enough fuel for the whole trip awaited us.

We ran into trouble immediately. Our Tibetan interpreter's "wrong" attitude angered the Chinese border police, who closed the office and went back to their quarters. We were forced to spend two unscheduled nights in Zhangmu. To make up for lost time, we skipped a day of acclimatization and went straight over a 5,050-meter (16,600-foot) mountain pass to reach the Tibetan Plateau.

At the day's end we pitched our tents on an open plain where strong winds blew. I suffered terribly from altitude sickness and spent the whole night vomiting. There is no cure for altitude sickness except to descend, but that was impossible. In front of us stretched the vast plateau, and to the east in the dying light rose the red peaks of Cho Oyu (8,153 metres, 26,155 feet), eighth highest peak in the world. Without taking out my camera I simply kept looking at the glorious sight, while trying to fight the nausea.

Early the next morning a long, strange shadow formed on the slopes of a bare hill, created by the sharp dawn rays. I had witnessed such scene before in deserts, but here the air's thinness enhanced the phenomenon.

Startled by the sound of our vehicles, a profusion of wild rabbits came running out from all directions and darted away. After this abrupt and unexpected vision, I lapsed into a reverie that contained an after-image of what I had just seen; it gave me some relief. My nausea and headache showed no sign of getting better and my hands and face had become swollen. The altitude sickness stayed with me for ten more unrelenting days and when it was finally over I had lost seven kilograms.

On the third day of our journey we reached the Changthang Plateau, a huge, desolate area in northwest Tibet known as the world's highest desert. With an average altitude of 4,900 metres (16,000 feet), it is beyond the reach of the monsoon rains and even grass finds it difficult to grow in the harsh climate.

In the sky we saw those curious round clouds sometimes depicted in Tibetan religious paintings and the weather fascinated us with its quick changes and wild force. On occasion, even when the sky was clear, we would experience sudden snowfalls and the giant snowflakes would blur our visibility. We continued to pass scenes so fantastic that I doubted what I was seeing was true.

As we crossed the plateau our Tibetan driver put on a much played cassette tape. There was a quiet narration and then a man started singing a sad Tibetan melody. Casually our driver and another of the Tibetans started to sing too. The song had three verses. When the song ended our Tibetan interpreter explained what it meant:

'This is a sad song about two brothers in the past who had to face their destiny. In the first verse the elder brother sings to his younger brother: "I must go to a foreign land. Younger brother, do not feel sad for it is my fate. There will be days when the sun will shine through the clouds." In the second verse, the younger sings to the elder: "I will stay behind. Elder brother, please do not feel sad, this also is my fate. For even a drop of water must flow to the great sea." In the third verse, the people sing to the two brothers: "We will accept this sadness, for this also is our fate. Please do not feel sad, for we are made well by the grace of you two brothers, who are like the Sun and the Moon." The elder brother is the 14th Dalai Lama and the younger one the Panchen Lama, who passed away in January 1989.'

This song was composed by exiled Tibetans and was secretly brought into Tibet. When the driver realized that we sympathized with Tibet's cause, he played the song at least once a day. As we continued our journey over endless rough roads the sad voice on the tape made us feel as though we were listening to the cry of Tibet, a land that was being trampled by the communists who have no sentiment or belief in religion.

On the evening of the seventh day after our departure from Zhangmu, we finally saw Mount Kailash. At first it looked like an insignificant and inconspicuous peak shaped like a peculiar pyramid. When we arrived in front of Kailash's south side, we got out of the vehicle. So this was the mysterious mountain! In fact, we were soon mesmerized by it and kept looking at the miraculous-looking summit shining in the sun. Deep down we felt a sense of

A thangka painting from Tragyam Monastery in Nepal shows the Kailash pilgrimage route and Lake Manasarowar. The temples painted on the thangka were all destroyed during the Cultural Revolution, but some are now being rebuilt.

warm ecstasy and identified strongly with the pilgrims who were prostrating and praying all around us. One and all had reached their destination.

About 500 tents were pitched at Dharchen in the foothills of Mount Kailash. This was the base camp for pilgrims and more than 5,000 had gathered there. Every day, many open trucks packed with new pilgrims would arrive and the tent town kept expanding.

One night I was awakened very late by the sound of footsteps. Pilgrims on the move! My watch showed it was just past one in the morning, and in wonder I listened to the faithful trudging off into the cold darkness.

Most pilgrims started early in the morning in order to complete the clockwise circumambulation of Mount Kailash in a single day. The 52-kilometre route took about 15 hours; pilgrims returned exhausted but happy, their faces reddened by the evening sun. After taking two or three days rest they would circle Kailash again.

For those of us suffering from the altitude and gasping for oxygen like goldfish, completing the circuit around the holy mountain in one day was out of the question. We hired eight porters and decided to make one circumambulation in four days. The porters were young Khampa men who had come on a pilgrimage from Kham Province in eastern Tibet. Khampas are robust and known for their rough temperament. Our men had already been in the Kailash region for over three months, and when I visited Kailash again the following year I was very surprised to see one of them still on his pilgrimage.

Buddhists always move in a clockwise direction when circling a sacred object, be it a statue in a temple or a mighty mountain. So of course we did likewise, and in the beginning the route was not very difficult. But every time we reached an incline we started to pant violently. After some time we reached a place with an excellent view of Mount Kailash, so we decided to make camp. We had pitched our tents and were resting when the porters came asking if we had any extra blankets. How absurd! They knew we would be spending freezing nights at altitudes up to 5,000 metres (16,400 feet), yet none of them bothered to bring proper bedding. Finally they took the bags and sacks in which we had brought our tents and other equipment and headed for the rocks to spend a shivering, miserable night. Much later I was awakened by the sound of something repeatedly hitting the tent; it was a hail storm.

The following morning, shortly after we had started walking, many pilgrims came one after the other and their numbers increased as they overtook us. They had set out from Dharchen before dawn and planned to return in the evening. They carried nothing but tsampa (roasted barley flour) for lunch and for all the world resembled city businessmen going to work, walking briskly and silently. Along the pilgrim route were many sacred sites. Footprints on all four sides of Kailash are said to be from the Buddha himself, and many others are impressions left behind by Tibetan saints. Stone depressions did indeed look like footprints and shone black from the touch of countless pilgrims.

On the third day we reached Kailash's northern side and witnessed a scene where a man was stuck in a gap between two rocks. People were trying to pull him free, and they finally succeeded. The big hapless man was utterly exhausted; he had tried unsuccessfully to pass through a gap in the 'sin-testing rocks'. It is said that only those free of sin (or very thin) can pass with no problem.

We met men and women progressing along the route by doing full-body prostrations, and many of them were young girls. I was astounded and breathless at the sight; there are no words to describe the heartfelt feelings that I experienced. I experienced a different kind of breathlessness, and throbbing hardship, while ascending the steep, snowy ravines of the 5,636-metre (18,491-foot) Dolma La pass. A mother carrying a baby on her back passed me with an expression as if to say; "What's the matter?" when she saw me stopping so frequently and gasping for breath. Pilgrims say that the greater the hardship, the greater the merit gained. I have no doubt that I earned a large amount of merit during my one circuit of Mount Kailash.

We returned to base camp to await the Saga Dawa festival, but unexpected trouble occurred. Local organisers absolutely forbade us to take photographs, and despite our protests and negotiations we failed to change their minds. The reason for no photographs was to protect pilgrims and organisers from being identified in case disturbances erupted during the festival. In the end we decided to leave without waiting for Saga Dawa. Soon after our departure, at a curve near a river bank, I was speechless upon seeing an appalling sight: There before us were 20 military trucks lined up with soldiers of the People's Liberation Army camping alongside them.

Sacred Mount Kailash was being surrounded by the military.

Lake Manasarowar lies at 4,558 metres (14,950 feet) above sea level and is known to the Tibetans as Mapham Tso.

A pilgrim begins his day by chanting scriptures at first light.

These rocks are said to have been piled on top of each other during the titanic struggle between Milarepa and his arch rival Narobonchung, over who had the right to Mount Kailash. Milarepa (1040–1123), Tibet's most revered poet-saint, was the victor.

# Tibet: Mountains and Plateaux

In geological terms, the creation of the Himalayas and the rising of the Tibetan Plateau are extremely recent events; the mountains are among the youngest in the world.

The violent creation of mountains and plateaux can be explained fairly simply. About 80 million years ago India broke away from an ancient massive proto-continent. It moved slowly and steadily northward, across the Sea of Tethys, collecting hard sheets of rock on its way. Eventually it rammed into the soft underside of Asia, which the harder rock easily penetrated and heaved up, creating the Himalayas. From sea level the mountains rose rapidly to a height of nearly 9,000 metres (30,000 feet). Today, the succession of parallel ranges, running west to east for nearly 3,200 kilometres (2,000 miles), reveals this original plate boundary between India and early Asia. In fact, the mass of sub-continental India is still forcing the Himalayas upwards at the remarkable rate of several centimetres a year, continually lifting Tibet's huge tableland by the constant pressure of the earth.

By far the largest natural region in Tibet is the Changthang, or Northern Plain, an enormous expanse of over 1,000,000 square kilometres (386,100 square miles) that covers almost half of Tibet's total surface area. It has undoubtedly one of the world's harshest climates, with strong winds every day and bitterly cold temperatures throughout the year.

Most of the Changthang is never visited by people, yet it is here, amidst nature's great desolation and isolation, that we find Mount Kailash, focus of so much human faith, hope and adoration.

A nomad woman of the Changthang region milks sheep tied together with a single rope. The sheep are used to being confined and do not struggle.

Nomads return home after the Gola Festival in Ngaba. This area of northwestern Sichuan Province lies at 3,500 metres (11,500 feet) and has plenty of rainfall, making it one of Tibet's greenest regions.

A nomad camp with fluttering prayer flags near Mount Kailash. The sky is darkened by monsoon clouds but it seldom rains.

Mother and child in the
Changthang region. The black tent,
woven from yak's hair, retains heat
well and the fire is fuelled by dried
animal dung, held here in a metal
basin.

*(Clockwise from top-left)*

Collecting yak dung is solely the preserve of women. The dung is dried flat and stored until needed as fuel.

These young herders in western Tibet have just returned from tending to the sheep.

Frost collects on a sleeping boy's shoulders. However cold the winter may be, young men and boys take turns staying up all night to look after the cattle.

Changthang nomads take sheep and goats to pasture after milking. The animals are grazed all day long because of scarce pasturage.

A nomad from Ngaba with his motorbike. These people live relatively close to Chengdu, capital of Sichuan Province, and profit from the sale of their yaks. They are better off than the Chinese farmers who live on narrow strips of land in the mountain valleys below the high plateau.

Nomad children in northern
Nagchu, near Amdo, on a cold
November evening.

*(Right)*
A boy leans against the sun-dried
bricks of his home. The nomads of
Nagchu have access to pastures
even in winter, so they can live in
houses rather than tents.

*(Above)*
Harsh pastureland in the Tingri region near Mount Everest in early winter. Strong winds blow continuously on winter afternoons in this mountainous region. The cattle survive on the little dry grass left on the barren hillsides.

*(Left)*
Grasslands of Kham (eastern Tibet) beneath dramatic cirrus clouds in late autumn. The region stands at 3,500 metres (11,500 feet) above sea level.

Dawn at a nomad camp, Ngaba region of northwestern Sichuan Province.

*(Above)*
Nomads circumambulate a hillside stupa in the Nagchu region continuously for an entire day to gain merit for themselves. They also seek good fortune and health for their beasts by driving them around and around in circles.
Some people ride bicycles, others ride in trucks to perform this essential Tibetan custom of circling holy sites.

*(Right)*
The Lhabab Duchen Festival is held on the twenty-second day of the ninth month according to the Tibetan calendar. It is said that on this day Gautama Buddha descended from the Thirty Three Heaven, where he had been giving teachings to his mother, according to his promise to her made before he attained enlightenment. Nomads circumambulate a stupa on a hill in the Nagchu region continuously for a day. Every year before the festival, starting from the Potala Palace, every Tibetan home is painted white with lime to welcome Lord Buddha.

*(Previous Pages)*
Mount Everest, the world's highest peak, rises on the left and Cho Oyu, eighth highest, stands on the right. On a very cold winter night the sun's afterglow seems not to fade even after the moon has risen.

*(Right)*
In mid-November, when temperatures can plummet to -20°C, two men wake up after a night in the open.

Horses drink water from a frozen stream. Like other Central Asian horses, they are small but very hardy.

Drawing water early in the morning by breaking ice, near Nagchu. In winter the nomads living in tents have a tough life. Without yak dung, the only source of fuel, they would not be able to survive.

*(Above)*
A young herder swings an urdo, the Tibetan sling. Hurled stones startle wandering sheep and bring them back to the fold. The basket on the boy's back is used for collecting yak dung.

*(Left)*
A sheep breeding camp at a pass 4,800 metres (15,750 feet) above sea level, near Tingri. It is winter and the young men have gathered their sheep from a village at the foot of the distant mountains.

Herders at a sheep station near Tingri. They eat only two meals a day, in the morning and evening. Their fare consists of tsampa, yogurt and butter tea. From sunrise to sunset they walk in the cold wind, following the sheep as they search for grass.

Herders waking up. They sleep
wrapped in furs with their heads
completely covered.

Members of a salt caravan in the
Phenpo region. A journey from the
salt lake on the high Changthang
plateau to Lhasa takes about three
months. The caravan walks for
about five hours in the morning
and then, because grass is scarce,
allows the yaks to spend the rest of
the day grazing. When the caravan
stops the men search for yak dung
fuel and set up camp.

Nomads slaughter a large number of livestock as winter draws near. A sacred drink is poured down the animal's throat, a short spell is chanted and then it is killed, either by suffocation or having the arteries to the heart severed by a knife.

*(Right)*
Meat becomes frozen and dried naturally in nomadic regions. At Yanspin in Qinghai Province a man carries part of a carcass on the first stage of its trip to Lhasa's markets. Dried yak meat fetches a better price than beef or mutton.

A nomad caravan from Ngaba
moves to higher pastures during the
summer. The caravan includes
more than 1,000 sheep and about
200 yaks. On the grasslands are a
few scattered villages where most
nomads spend their winters.

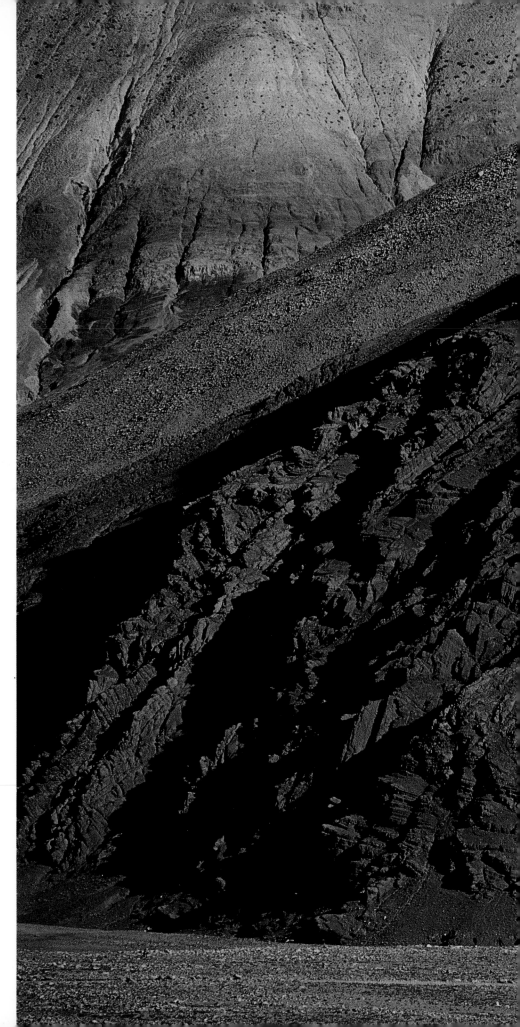

*(Above)*
A hot spring geyser in western Tibet. The Himalayas are still geologically unstable so hot springs occur in a few places in Tibet.

*(Right)*
Exposed rock near Mount Everest. A hundred million years ago, before the Indian and Eurasian land masses collided and caused the great uplifting of the earth's crust that formed the Himalayas, the Tibetan plateau was the bed of the Sea of Tethys. This primordial sea is mentioned in Tibetan creation myths.

*(Previous Pages)*
The Yarlung Tsangpo, Tibet's most important river, originates near Mount Kailash. It flows from west to east until cutting a dramatic gorge through the Himalayas to reach India, at which point it becomes the Brahmaputra. Here, southeast of Lhasa, the calm water reflects November clouds.

*(Above)*
The rare blue poppy is found only in the Himalayas. The flower becomes shorter as the altitude increases; this specimen is at 5,300 metres (17,400 feet), near the plant's uppermost limit.

*(Right)*
The Kyichu Valley near Lhasa in summer, Tibet's most beautiful season. Summer lasts for about three months, after which the land becomes brown and desolate.

A barley harvest in Gyantse. The barley is reaped in August and September and then dried. Before it is winnowed, cattle walk over the grains so the chaff can be more easily separated. Tsampa, Tibet's staple food, is ground roasted barley flour.

A harvest scene in the Phenpo region. The barley here is a hardy strain that can grow up to 4,000 metres (13,200 feet). After the harvest and grain preparation, many villagers go on pilgrimages.

A beam of sunlight enters a smoke-filled room where villagers enjoy tea.

*(Above)*
An old man drinks a cup of butter tea. The tea is prepared by boiling tea leaves, then straining the liquid and mixing it with salt and butter. The taste is more like soup than tea.

*(Right)*
Magnificent stone houses stand in a fertile valley of the Ngaba region. The ground floor of each house is a cattle shed, the first and second floors are living quarters and the third floor is the prayer hall.

(Above)
A primary school in Dingri. The teaching materials are old and worn out but portraits of the 'great revolutionaries' of China are brand new.

(Right)
These youngsters, separated from their parents in the hills, live and study at a boarding school. One source claims only about 20 percent of children attend primary school in the Tibet Autonomous Region. Some parents, despairing for their children's education, secretly send them to India to study at schools run by the exiled Tibetan Government.

*(Top-left)*
Soldiers of the People's Liberation Army buy meat from a Muslim butcher in Lhasa. Since Tibetans have religious scruples about killing animals, all the slaughtering in Lhasa is done by Muslims.

*(Above)*
Pilgrims burn incense in front of Lhasa's Jokhang Temple and throw bundles of paper with Buddha images on them into the air.

*(Left)*
Butter is commonly stored and preserved in the stomach of a yak or other animal.

A nomad woman looks at beads
and necklaces at a stall on the
Barkhor, the pilgrim route around
the Jokhang Temple.

# Living with the Yaks

In July 1989 I was following the route taken by Mao Tse-tung and his Red Army during the Long March of 1935. In that epic struggle for survival the communists passed through the remote and rugged region of Ngaba in Tibet, which today is incorporated within Sichuan Province of China. The province is famous for its poor weather, to such a point that 'dogs bark at the unfamiliar sun'. In early summer, heat and rain are a daily oppression.

On one such day I finally received a travel permit to enter the Ngaba region, so immediately I chartered a four-wheel-drive vehicle and headed for the high plateau. After eight hours on the road through deep gorges, past rushing rivers, I climbed above the forest and suddenly found myself in a vast grassland 3500 metres above sea level.

In a moment the world turned from gray to gold and green. Cumulonimbus clouds rose in the sky and rays of sunlight shone from the blue heavens. Endless hills were covered with glorious blossoms of every imaginable color. Men on horseback tended large herds that ambled towards their summer pastures. One herd had hundreds of yaks and thousands of sheep, bringing to mind great expeditions of another age. Yet even such vast numbers of animals seemed like ants crawling in the grasslands when seen from even a short distance.

The thin air made me dizzy; the beautiful scene seemed like a scroll painting etched into my aching head. I did not think it possible that such a serene land could exist next to the dense, overpopulated Chinese world with its rice fields, noise and toil. But the two entirely different cultures do stand side by side, separated by nature's barrier of 3000-meter altitude.

In a village along the broad valley it was the time of year for viewing flowers. The villagers had pitched tents on the grasslands and were eating, drinking, singing and enjoying the short season of blooms. Though poor in material goods, the people were generous and carefree, an attitude to life I have rarely seen among Chinese farmers.

In the valleys and along slopes the local folk erected white flags and banners. When I looked more closely I saw that the flags were printed with prayers. The noise made by flapping was loud and mesmerizing. Though I was standing alone in a wilderness, these emblems of devotion gave me the eerie feeling of the presence of praying people. It was as though the flags were trying to catch the wind and prove to the skies that humans existed all around. In fact the wind reads the prayers and carries them to the gods above.

In the late afternoon, as usual, there was lightning and thunder and strong gusts of wind. A strong shower attacked the paradise where skylarks wheeled and butterflies danced. Soon the rain clouds disappeared and blue skies returned. At night the cycle of changing weather repeated itself and at dawn the ground was covered with a thin layer of ice from the wet chill of the dark hours. It was the same pattern every day. Nature in all its guises allowed me to escape the world's confusion. In Tibet I discovered a land where I could not help but feel the presence of the Omnipotent.

Daily attuned in this way to the glories of the grasslands, I came to know Tibet; what irony that I sought the roots of the Chinese revolution! And in contrast to the journalists of the Long March, who described swamps, hardships and frightening desolation, I was totally enchanted with the grand and free grasslands and these upland people.

In November 1992 I stood on the Thang La Pass at 5,231 metres above sea level, the highest point on the road that links Qinghai Province and Lhasa away to the south. This pass was once the main obstacle on the caravan route to the capital, but now the road makes the journey quite easy. Still, in spite of only a gentle breeze and light, wafting clouds, it was very cold.

Five thousand metres is considered to be the limit of normal daily life for humans, and even the nomads spend only part of the year at this altitude. After a month I am usually well acclimatized though I sometimes unconsciously breathe deeply, and nighttime is always a small ordeal with the extremely cold temperatures, often -20 degrees C. With four blankets over my sleeping bag I was somehow able to bear the cold, though in the mornings the inside of my tent and the top of my head would be covered with ice and frost.

A lake nearly 100 metres in diameter stood near the road in a region devoid of any living beings. The surface was covered with thick ice, and as I looked at the lake I suddenly became aware of dark shadows moving about. Were they not children playing? I stopped the vehicle and went down to the lake, whereupon I saw three tents pitched near a hill to avoid the late-autumn winds. The figures did prove to be children, sisters playing together. They placed a baby on an old pan, used as a sled, which they pulled around on the ice with a rope. The children were wrapped in thick fur, their cheeks a deep red from the cold. When I saw their joyful faces I marveled at the resourcefulness and greatness of humanity. Here were people who had almost nothing, living in an oxygen-depleted environment; yet the children were being brought up happily.

From one of the tents came the sound of prayers. As I approached a man with unkempt hair peeped out and with a smile invited me in. The prayers came from an old woman who sat facing the family shrine inside the tent. She continued to pray without paying any attention to me. A young woman, the mother of the children outside, turned a

Men treat a pony attacked by a wolf.

Even today nomads use harquebuses for hunting. This man boasted that he could bring down a deer from 150 paces.

Tsampa, the ever-present staple food of Tibetans, is mixed with butter tea, kneaded and eaten.

stone mill to grind roasted barley into tsampa, the staple food of all Tibetans. A strange harmony existed between the sound of the prayers and the sound of the stone mill. As I watched the mill turning round and round I thought of the wheel of karma and the cycle of existence that binds all living beings, and in this isolated spot on the planet I felt warmed and humbled. The old woman steadily turned a prayer wheel in her right hand and with the thumb of her left hand she thoughtfully moved each bead of her rosary.

The quiet strength of these people suits the hard, free life of the nomad. It is a life of close dependence on the yak, a beast that is adapted perfectly to the cold and high altitude of Tibet. It provides clothes, food, shelter and fuel; here, life for humans would be impossible without the yak.

In the center of all tents in this land, the hearth is a heater as well as a stove. There is little actual living space, as so much room is taken up by dried yak dung, piled high and picked at constantly to feed the fire. The dung burns at a low temperature but it burns well for a long time.

The best clothing for the Tibetan winter is a coat called paktsa, made from the furry hide of the yak. Coracles for crossing rivers and lakes are also made from yak hides stitched together and stretched over a wooden framework. Tents are made of felt or woven strands of yak hair, perfect for the harsh conditions. Their black color absorbs heat, keeping the tents warm during the day, and their porous nature allows good ventilation, keeping the rain out.

The nomads' diet consists mostly of dairy products and yak meat. Dried meat hangs in the corner of a tent and needs no cooking, naturally preserved by air and smoke. Tea prepared with butter and salt is drunk many times a day and provides the main source of hydration and nutrition for Tibetans. Tsampa roasted barley flour is bought or bartered to round out the diet.

There is virtually no waste in the life of the nomads. Everything is used, consumed or recycled. Perhaps the most remarkable example of returning all things to the cycle of life is the way human corpses are treated. In the ritual of 'sky-burial', the body is cut into little pieces and the bones and skull are crushed to allow vultures, kites and other birds to consume all parts. Even death fits into the ecosystem of the Tibetan Plateau.

One day I visited a sky-burial site after the solemn ritual. I waited until the area was free of people, then approached fearfully with my Tibetan guide. The site commanded a good view halfway up a mountain. The huge flat rock used to dismember the body was entirely sprinkled with white tsampa flour, an act done to purify the blood and other remains of the funeral. I was touched by the sight of some sweet sparrows innocently pecking at the tsampa. A little distance away on a hill the contented vultures rested and looked down upon us. This gave me an uneasy feeling, and I tried to remind myself of the Buddhist concepts of impermanence and compassion for all beings. Then my eyes fell on the hammer and hatchet used to break the skulls of dead humans and I could no longer remain calm; it was hard to accept the fact that a man had just been broken into pieces and fed to those vultures up above.

In the last hours of one's life, monks pray and try to bring one to a place of equipoise where the continuous cycle of rebirth and death is understood and faced without fear. Once the karma-bearing soul leaves the body of a human, the physical remains are not important and can be used to nurture further life; in this case the birds. Tibetans have believed and practiced this for generations, thus creating a kind of ecosystem of the heart that fits beautifully into the life of the high plateau.

# Days of Tibetan Buddhism

Recorded history in Tibet begins with the reign of King Songtsen Gambo (ca. 617–698 C.E.), a young warrior king who unified all Tibet and made Lhasa his capital. The introduction of Buddhism also dates from the 7th century, and is usually attributed to the influence of the king's two main foreign wives. Songtsen Gambo posed enough of a threat to China that he could demand a Chinese princess as a bride. The Emperor Tai Tsung, first of the Tang Dynasty, sent his adopted daughter, Wen Cheng, to Tibet with much pomp and ceremony and a gold Buddha statue as her dowry. It is said that the country's most sacred statue, the venerable image of Sakyamuni Buddha in the Jokhang, is the very one brought by Wen Cheng 1,350 years ago. The king made another alliance by marrying Princess Tritsun of Nepal. His three Tibetan wives gave birth to the children who continued Tibet's Yarlung Dynasty.

After Songtsen Gampo, the first "Religious King", four generations of kings devoted themselves to the expansion of the Tibetan empire and the nurturing of Buddhism. The new faith made headway by replacing the old Bon religion with the help of Indian Tantrism, a development of monastic and Mahayana Buddhism that harnessed esoteric and magical elements to the Buddhist ideals of liberation and universal positive evolution. The tradition brought to Tibet a written language system, the profound learning accumulated over centuries in India, an inspiring religious worldview, and the peaceful social ethic needed to temper the Tibetan warrior spirit of those times.

Tibet's first monastery, Samye, was founded towards the end of the 8th century by Trisong Detsen, the second main "Religious King", after he had invited prominent Buddhists from India to come and teach. The most famous were Padmasambhava, a great Tantric magician-saint, and Santarakshita, a learned monastic sage and Mahayana philosopher. Both helped found Samye Monastery as a school to train Tibetan monks, modelling it after a monastery in India. Hundreds of volumes of Indian Buddist scriptures and treatises were carefully translated into Tibetan.

A sheep is suffocated by tying a rope tightly around its mouth. This method prevents any loss of precious blood, which is used for stuffing sausages.

The peculiar Tibetan greeting—a man sticks out his tongue to show it is not black (the tongue of a poisoner is believed to be black) and displays his palms to show he has no hidden weapons.

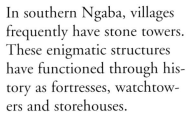

In southern Ngaba, villages frequently have stone towers. These enigmatic structures have functioned through history as fortresses, watchtowers and storehouses.

Trisong Detsen proclaimed Buddhism the official religion of Tibet, upon which two of his five queens and 300 other people promptly took religious vows and joined holy orders.

Despite these early successes, Buddhism did face resistance from the indigenous Bon religion. Most of the aristocracy clung tenaciously to the old faith and hated the newly privileged class of monks, which they saw as a mortal threat to themselves and even to the monarchy. A crisis soon arrived that proved them correct.

In the middle of the 9th century Tri Ralwajen, the grandson of Trisong Detsen, turned over his whole administration to a monk. This blindly pious king was soon assassinated by his brother Lang Darma, who became infamous as the grand persecutor of Buddhism. He set out to extinguish the religion entirely; monasteries and temples were systematically disbanded, monks were killed and dispersed, and Buddhism in Tibet went into eclipse for more than 100 years. King Lang Darma himself was murdered by an avenging monk and with that the monarchy came to an end. The country collapsed into enclaves ruled by different groups.

Gradually, peace returned and Buddhism slowly came back, especially in West Tibet under the Guge Kingdom. Atisha, a famous 11th-century monk, sage, and Tantric master from India, journeyed northward just when Tibet was ready for a religious revival. Under his influence Tibetans formed communities to study aspects of Buddhist doctrine and practice. Monasteries sprang up and there arose the many orders, or schools, of Tibetan Buddhism, known by the color of their hats. 'Red Hats' and 'Black Hats' were strongest, though for nearly 400 years rivalries and power struggles for the control of Tibet persisted.

Into this situation came a saintly scholar named Tsong Khapa (1357–1419), Tibet's great reformer. He founded Ganden Monastery near Lhasa and established a new order, the 'Yellow Hats'. Strict morality, celibacy, and a purified doctrine that followed Atisha's teachings marked the Yellow Hat monks. Tsong Khapa's disciples founded Lhasa's huge monasteries of Sera and Drepung and popularized their master's philosophical and religious writings. The Yellow Hat order eventually became Tibet's most popular Buddhist movement.

One line of Yellow Hat reincarnate abbots became known as the "Dalai Lamas" (Oceanic Masters). There have been fourteen such men who have ruled in an unbroken line of succession since the coronation of the Great Fifth in 1642. The title "Dalai", or "Ocean" (Ocean of Wisdom) was given to the Third Dalai Lama in 1578 by a Mongol king, and applied posthumously to the first two. The Great Fifth, who unified Tibet and built the Potala Palace, was recognized with his four predecessors and all future Dalai Lamas as Avalokiteshvara, the Bodhisattva of Compassion, and thus believed to possess divine status.

When a Dalai Lama died, a search for his reincarnation began at once. Helped by the State Oracle, portents and dreams, high lamas searched the country for a boy with special physical traits, such as long eyes and large ears, who, in addition to other tests, could identify the late Dalai Lama's possessions among a pile of similar objects.

The unique institution of incarnations developed in Tibet's distinctive form of Buddhism, considered a synthesis of monastic, messianic, and Tantric Buddhisms. The Dalai Lamas are simply the highest level of the reincarnations; throughout the Tibetan world there have been more than several thousand such lineages. Labrang Tashikyil Monastery alone had more than 50 recognized reincarnations.

The Great Fifth and the Thirteenth (1876–1933) were historically the most important Dalai Lamas, men of great personal power and administrative ability. The Thirteenth Dalai Lama, for all his strengths, was unable to get the British to introduce Tibet into world recognition in the League of Nations, nor could he bring about the various reforms he envisioned to modernize the nation. Indeed, when the Chinese communists won their revolution in 1949 and then turned their attention to Tibet the following year, the Tibetans were wholly unable to resist being taken over.

In 1959 the present Dalai Lama was forced into exile, yet for these 35 years he has remained the focus and hope of the Tibetan people. If anything, their feelings for him have only grown stronger as he upholds the faith and preaches peace and non-violence in his adopted land. The torch of Buddhism that was once carried into Tibet from India more than 1,200 years ago has now once again crossed the Himalayas and lives on in India.

Monlam, the Great Prayer Festival, starts on the first day of the Tibetan New Year and continues for about three weeks. At the Monlam held at Labrang Tashikyil Monastery in Gansu Province, a huge applique thangka is unfurled in front of devotees. The Buddha is the centerpiece.

Two pilgrims from Ngaba head for the holy city of Lhasa. They will prostrate the entire way and their remarkable pilgrimage of 1,800 kilometres (1,100 miles) will take four years.

Pilgrims circle Labrang Tashikyil.
In the centre two people rotate
prayer wheels; inside these cylinders
are rolls of printed paper that bear
mantras or prayers. Tibetans believe
that one rotation of the wheel
equals a full recitation of the prayer.

A nomad father and son at the
Jokhang Temple, Tibet's most
important shrine. People of all
social classes and from all parts of
the country come to worship here.

*(Above)*
This statue of Sakyamuni, the historical Buddha, is the Jokhang Temple's main image. Every year the face is painted with gold. It is said that the statue was brought from China by the Tang Dynasty Princess Wen Cheng when she came to Tibet to marry King Songtsen Gampo in 640 AD. At this time Tibet was a military rival of the Tang.

*(Right)*
Pilgrims moving towards the sanctuary of the Jokhang Temple. The pilgrim in front is holding a khata (ceremonial scarf). Khatas are offered to high lamas and to important images while praying at sacred places.

(Above)
Young boys at Labrang Tashikyil
Monastery pray and prostrate on
the snow-covered ground.

(Right)
A young boy circumabulates
Labrang Tashikyil Monastery; the
circuit takes about 20 minutes to
complete along the outer pilgrim
route surrounding the huge temple
grounds.

*(Left)*
Monks called Geko maintain order during the Monlam, as well as carrying incense in front of a procession of high lamas to cleanse the way. The decorations on this monk's back symbolize his status as Geko.

*(Above)*
Geko monks in front of a white wall. Before annexation by China, Monlam was held on a large scale in Lhasa and during the festival the government handed over the responsibility for maintaining order to the monk-police.

*(Above)*
An old woman walks past a gathering of monks during the Monlam. Monlam is the largest Tibetan Buddhist festival, founded in Lhasa in 1409, and its purpose is to pray for world peace and prosperity. However, the 1988 Monlam in Lhasa was called off after monks protested against the government using the festival to promote tourism and it has not been held there since.

*(Right)*
Young monks watch a masked dance during the Monlam. Before the Chinese invasion about ten percent of the Tibetan population were monks. Now, the numbers permitted to become monks are tightly restricted by the Chinese.

The ritual cham dance is held on the fifteenth day of the first lunar month. It is a slow, rhythmic, masked dance intended to drive away evil spirits. It lasts for six hours and all the while pilgrims watch silently.

After the cham dance ends, monks line up to burn a ritual effigy symbolizing all the evil aspects of the past year.

A row of long-handled langa drums
display wrathful guardian deities.
The drums are used during religious festivals and, with cymbals,
during daily religious services.

A huge thangka unfurled on the slopes of a hill above Labrang. The devotees, who have been waiting for hours to see it, have begun to offer white khata scarves, which accumulate at the thangka's base.

*(Above)*
Monks carry the huge rolled thang-ka downhill after it has been shown to the public. This thangka is only shown once in a year during the Monlam Festival.

*(Left)*
After the ceremony many believers press their foreheads to the chair recently occupied by Jamyang Shayba Rinpoche, a holy personage. Jamyang Shayba has been the name of Labrang Tashikyil's reincarnated chief abbot since the 17th century. Devotees later rushed to touch the Rinpoche's jeep with their hands and foreheads.

*(Above)*
Kasarpani Avalokiteshvara painted
on a wall of the Jokhang Temple in
17th century classical style. It is
believed that the Dalai Lamas are
incarnations of Avalokiteshvara, the
Bodhisattva of Compassion, who
descended to earth to save
mankind.

*(Left)*
Mandala palace and surrounding
universe of the Buddha Vairochana,
painted on the wall of a fifth-floor
chapel inside the Great Stupa of
Gyantse. Surrounding the central
mandala are a thousand Buddhas
depicted as fierce deities.

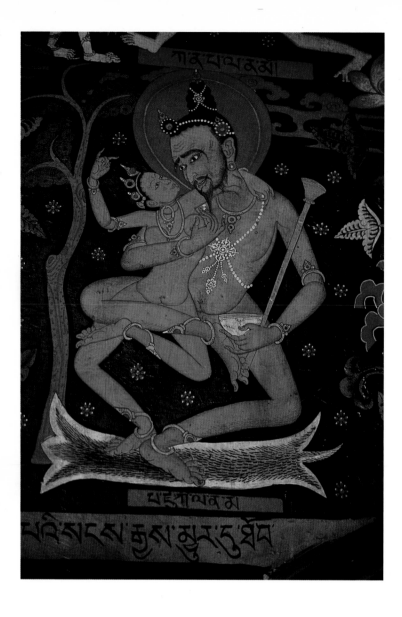

*(Top-left)*
A fresco painting from Palkor Chode Monastery in Gyantse. It shows Pajuka, one of the 84 tantric Adepts of ancient India, and his female partner. At that time sexual union was practised as a springboard to attain the tantric, or yogic, realization of Buddhahood as the non-duality of bliss and voidness.

*(Top-right)*
Detail of a Buddhadakini (female Buddha-deity) stepping on a mundane goddess (her previous self as an unenlightened being), from a seventh-floor chapel of the Great Stupa of Gyantse.

*(Bottom)*
An image of a multi-armed form of White Tara at Shar Temple.

*(Right)*
A wall painting at Toling Temple, western Tibet, shows the daughter of one of the eight naga kings described in the Lotus Sutra paying homage to the Buddha. Nagas are water deities, widely worshipped as rain-makers.

*(Previous Pages)*
Nomads on horseback line up to welcome a revered incarnation (tulku) who has come to perform a religious ceremony in the Ngaba region.

*(Right)*
A crowd of 5,000 gathers to hear the teachings of the reincarnation, Dragyab Rinpoche, who usually lives in exile in Germany. He is seated on a throne with ritual bell, drum and dorje (thunderbolt) before him.

*(Left)*
A group of pilgrims heading from Ngaba to Lhasa stop for lunch. The man offers tea to the gods before drinking it himself.

*(Above)*
In a village near Shigatse, people bid farewell to a high monk by throwing tsampa into the air.

*(Above)*
Villagers watch a cham dance at the Zonze Temple, the first such performance here in 40 years.

*(Left)*
At Zonze Temple near Gyantse villagers and pilgrims receive free food during a festival. The temple, destroyed during the Cultural Revolution, was rebuilt after seven years of voluntary labour by the villagers.

Drepung Monastery just west of Lhasa was established in 1416 by Jamyang Chojey, a disciple of Tsong Khapa, founder of the Gelugpa, (Yellow Hat) Order of Tibetan Buddhism. Drepung, one of three huge Yellow Hat monasteries in the Lhasa area (the other two are Sera and Ganden), escaped total destruction in the 1960s because the People's Liberation Army used part of it as an army base. However, all Buddha images inside were destroyed.

The Great Stupa of Gyantse with the Palkor Chode Monastery to the right. The stupa, known as Kumbum (Place of Ten-thousand Images), records within its 75 chapels and temples practically the whole pantheon of Indo-Tibetan religion up to the time of its construction during the first half of the 15th century.

*(Left)*
Monks of Tashilhunpo
Monastery in Shigatse chop
mutton. Tibetans consider
killing animals unethical, though
they still eat meat. Climate, altitude and limited diet make vege-
tarianism nearly impossible.

*(Right-top)*
Two nuns print Buddhist scriptures at the Ani Tsangkung
Nunnery in Lhasa by using the
age-old method of wood block
printing.

*(Right-bottom)*
The hands of a nun hold the
loose leaves of a scripture-book,
known in Tibetan as pecha.

At Palkor Chode Monastery in Gyantse a monk prays to the guardian deity while holding a skull-shaped vessel and bell.

Monks of Ganden Monastery
soothe their dry throats by drinking
tea after a religious service. The service was requested by a devotee
who will offer each monk 15 yuan
(US$2).

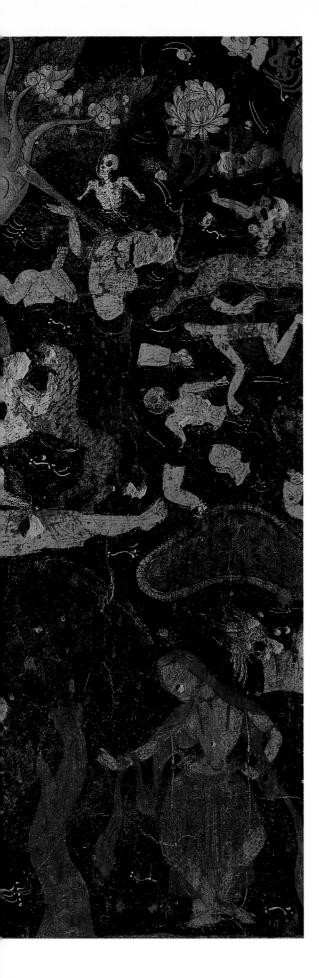

*(Above)*
The 'sky-burial' site near Sera Monastery in the suburbs of Lhasa. Here, corpses are cut up and broken to allow birds to eat the flesh. After the vultures have finished, tsampa is sprinkled on the site to cover the blood and other remains.

*(Left)*
Scenes from a charnel ground, painted on a wall of Toling Temple, western Tibet. Such depictions encourage non-attachment to the body.

*(Above)*
Dogs scavenge at a 'sky-burial' site behind the Jukun Temple in northeast Lhasa. Today non-Tibetans are strictly prohibited from going near such sites.

*(Left)*
The body of the tenth Panchen Lama, preserved and gilded, sits in state at Tashilhunpo Monastery, Shigatse. In August 1993, four-and-a-half years after his death, the Panchen Lama was enshrined in a stupa-tomb and can no longer be seen.

*(Above)*
Pilgrims at Palkor Chode Monastery in Gyantse. Tears fill the woman's eyes as she gazes at an image of Sakyamuni Buddha.

Three nuns circle huge rocks near the shore of sacred Lake Namtso, north of Lhasa. These rocks are considered the guardian deities of the lake; nearby a small cave monastery is called Tashi Do, Auspicious Rock.

On the high plateau, with the
Nyenchen Tanglha Range in the
background.

# Pure Land of the Butter Lamps

Throughout Tibet, in all its temples and monasteries, in front of every statue of the Buddha, before every image of a mythological or historical figure, are butter lamps. Some are huge, more than a metre in diameter, filled with butter and illuminated with many wicks of twisted cotton. Frequently, hundreds of lamps light a single room, and interiors of all buildings are redolent with the smell of grease and soot.

Streams of pilgrims all over the country bring their own butter to fuel the lamps in an age-old act of offering. Butter invariably spills so that the floors of any religious building are sticky and slippery and cause an unpleasant sensation when walking. But this is part of the pilgrim experience, as is contact with curtains, banners and embroidered cloth turned black and shiny with years of accumulated grease and dirt from handling.

Inside the temples is the unforgettable smell of ceaselessly burning lamps, a smell that many visitors consider the quintessence of Tibet. Then there are the innumerable Buddha statues glittering in the dim light, adding power and mystery to the atmosphere.

Most of Tibet's statues were destroyed in the 1950s and 1960s, requiring replacements to be made in the 1980s. In the rush to reconstruct, many were made clumsily and painted with bright, gaudy colors, lips scarlet and eyes glaring and vulgar. Old images of the Buddha were regularly given fresh coatings of gold paint. Some deserted temples were rebuilt to attract tourists and received kitsch decorations like those of a Chinese restaurant.

However, Tibetan pilgrims always come to temples with hearts full of earnestness and devotion. Many prostrate themselves along the butter-spattered pilgrim pathways while reciting prayers. In front of a statue of the Buddha they chant the sacred formula Om Mani Padme Hum and bare their hearts fully to the religious experience. The rugged Tibetans, toughened and trained by the severe climate of their remarkable, high-altitude land, pray with all their might in the temples and reveal an amplitude of faith and gentleness.

In Tibetan monasteries the main religious hall is accompanied by a smaller hall called the gonkhang, which houses the temple's guardian deity. This small hall has awesome power whereby concentrated, wrathful energy is directed against the enemies of Buddhism. I shall never forget the shock I received when I unknowingly stepped into a dim room in a corner of Palkor Chode Monastery in Gyantse. All four walls were completely covered with ghastly pictures of Hell. There were murals of the dead being dragged by their hair by horrid devils and birds pecking at corpses that were torn to pieces by wolves. Bodies were skewered, severed heads linked together to form necklaces, skull-goblets filled with blood. And at the main entrance was a huge statue of Lord Yamantaka, the horned, fanged bull, crushing a demon under foot, exercising its power as a protective deity. The statue was covered in layers of thin white scarves called khata, as if to calm down its fierceness and anger. From the soot-blackened ceiling stared down a row of grotesque ceremonial masks. In the Tibetan belief system, all of these powerful, frightening manifestations take on actual form and give reality to wrathfulness and death.

Tibetans jokingly explain about their habit of eating meat, in spite of being Buddhists, by referring to the ancient myth of their origin. The legend recounts that the first six Tibetans were offspring born of a monkey, the incarnation of Avalokiteshvara, Bodhisattva of Compassion, and a fierce ogress. Those who inherited the characteristics of the father are kind and intelligent and those who take after the mother are aggressive and have a liking for blood and meat. In fact, on the high plateau of Tibet it is difficult to grow vegetables and the diet has come to rely heavily on meat and dairy products. Precious blood is saved and used for filling sausages. Tibetans enjoy dried meat and do not worry that it is uncooked. During feasts and celebrations, nomads and villagers of rough exterior and warrior-like appearance sit cross-legged on the floor wearing fur caps. With small knives they cut off bite-sized pieces of meat from huge chunks of flesh attached to bones and put the meat into their mouths with the knives. The scene reminds one of the feast of ogresses.

In spite of this roughness, the kindness of Tibetans never fails to impress foreign visitors. In his book Seven Years in Tibet, the Austrian mountaineer Heinrich Harrer writes touchingly about how the Tibetans would make a big fuss and stop construction work to save an insect exposed while removing earth. People of this kind of sentiment could not bring themselves to slaughter cattle or other animals, so in the countryside there is a class of professional butchers known as shen-pa. In Lhasa, the work is done by Muslims.

Sometimes devout Tibetans will purchase and rescue an animal destined for the slaughterhouse and take care of it until it lives out its natural life span. If a family member is sick, a relative or sibling will save a sheep or cow in this way, believing the virtuous act will aid in the recovery of the bed-ridden person.

Dolma Taring (b. 1910) was the first Tibetan woman to study abroad in Darjeeling and to receive a Western education. In her autobiography, Daughter of Tibet, she writes that when a cow was being taken to the slaughterhouse, a person would offer money in exchange for the

The Wheel of Life, a pictorial allegory of Tibetan cosmology, shows the realms of demi-gods, hungry ghosts, hell-beings, animals, humans and gods. The entire depiction is held by Yama (Death), the Demon of Impermanence.

beast and ask the Muslim butcher to buy meat in the market instead. In this way the saviour and the butcher engage in meritorious acts.

Tibetans sometimes have a curious sense of value. They believe that large animals killed for food provide sustenance for many people, and therefore less bad karma is generated by one death than the killing of many smaller animals for the same volume of food.

In the olden days, the greatest fear among pilgrims and travelling merchants was the gangs of ruthless bandits that preyed on caravans. Chinese military rule has eradicated this menace, but nomads living in the mountains and salt traders who traverse huge distances still wear swords at their sides. They continue to project an image of untamed wildness.

During World War II, Hisao Kimura, a secret agent of the Japanese government, smuggled himself into Tibet and stayed there until several years after the war. In his book Ten Years Undercover in Tibet, he presents a striking aspect of the Tibetans. "The Mongolians say their prayers wholeheartedly and with complete devotion. The Tibetans living in the Lhasa area while saying their prayers will steal if nobody is around. The people of Amdo while saying their prayers steal openly, and the people of Kham while saying their prayers kill and steal . . ."

In the province of Kham there is a disturbing saying:

*'Without killing one cannot eat,*
*Without going to the temple one cannot lessen one's sins.*
*Kill a person . . . go to the temple.*
*Om Mani Padme Hum.'*

In another book, Tibet Travels by Ekai Kawaguchi, the author writes about a thief from Kham who travels to Mount Kailash to repent of his wrongdoing. He faces the holy mountain and shouts, "Oh! Khang Rinpoche, Precious Snow Mountain, Oh! Lord Buddha, Oh! Precious Three Jewels! Until today I have killed people, stolen many things, stolen other men's wives, fought with people. Here today I deeply repent for all these crimes, and now I truly believe all my sins have been forgiven. I will always repent here in advance for the killings, thefts and fights that I am going to perform in the future . . ."

Apparent callousness is part of the nature of some Tibetans, though most are truly gentle and life-affirming. This can be seen every day on the Barkhor, the circular street that surrounds Lhasa's Jokhang Temple. Pilgrims and traders congregate here from all over the country to create a colorful, rousing bazaar filled with religious artifacts, antiques, foodstuffs, clothes, leather goods, tools and household products of every description. Towards the end of October, when the demands of farming life slacken, the number of pilgrims increases greatly and they can be seen in droves circumambulating the sacred temple. Each circuit takes about fifteen minutes, and there exists a wonderful atmosphere of devotion, gaiety, laughter and commerce.

On the Barkhor one meets Tibetans from all walks and levels of society. Women of somewhat fair complexion, wearing their hair in 108 pleats and decked in bright clothing, come from the region of Amdo in the northeast. Men of Kham are strong and tall, easily recognized by the red tassel braided into their long hair. The tanned, small-statured men and women in simple attire are farmers from central Tibet. The exotic folk wearing peculiar brimless hats are from the Lopa and Monpa tribes in the far south where low altitudes and monsoons prevail. There are men in stately traditional clothes and women with overflowing amounts of jewellery as well as rustic nomad families making their first visit ever from the mountains to the bustle of Lhasa.

As evening draws near, the locals come out to join the scene, to stroll and chat and catch up on the day's gossip. Lhasans love the centre of their city and the unique atmosphere of the streets, always changing, always fun and stimulating. Pilgrims are here at all times, as are monks who chant loudly to collect donations. There are beggars as well, though most people soliciting money do it for a good cause, such as rebuilding a temple or small monastery.

Pilgrims frequently make small donations. Here and there are old people leading sheep that have been purchased and saved from the butcher's knife. As if knowing they can live out their lives in peace, the animals have serene faces like their aged masters.

In front of the Jokhang Temple is a courtyard of huge paving stones, and here many people make continuous, silent prostrations in the direction of the temple's closed gates. They are praying and honouring the image of Sakyamuni Buddha inside, Tibet's holiest statue. Centuries of full-body prostrations have made the stones shiny and slightly concave, and the devotions continue day after day. The stream of pilgrims to Lhasa seems endless, and in their numbers and in their faith one comes to know directly the great kindness of the Tibetan people, their compassion for all living things and the infinite hope for a good rebirth in the next life.

Prayer flags are strung in the configuration of a stupa at a sacred site in Ngaba, East Tibet.

Skull bowls, called kapala, sell for 100 yuan (US$12) at a souvenir shop in Lhasa. They are filled with water and offered at temple altars.

Monks pour tea (symbolizing animal blood) from a skull bowl to pacify evil spirits before performing a cham dance. This is an ancient custom that pre-dates the introduction of Buddhism to Tibet in the 7th century.

# Remains of the Guge Kingdom

Two hundred kilometres (125 miles) south of the Sutlej River in arid western Tibet, there is a broad wasteland with a deep fissure. Barren hills extend as far as the eye can see and it is here, in this forlorn landscape, that the ruins of the ancient Guge Kingdom lie.

From the 7th to the 9th century central Tibet was united under the Yarlung Dynasty. Buddhism was officially supported by the state and the new religion from India flourished until King Lang Darma, a follower of the indigenous Bon faith, came to power. He ruthlessly suppressed Buddhism. After an avenging monk killed Lang Darma, the dynasty collapsed and the ensuing power vacuum led to a period of confusion in Tibet. Under these unfavourable conditions, members of the aristocracy fled to western Tibet and built a kingdom called Guge. It prospered by being on an important Himalayan trade route.

In the 10th century, the great King Yeshe Ö reinstated Buddhism in this remote part of Tibet. He was helped tremendously by the brilliant translator and scholar Rinchen Zangpo, who promoted cultural exchanges with the Indian Buddhist world. Together they built over 100 monasteries, the most important being Toling which became the centre of Buddhist study in western Tibet. Buddhism further benefitted by the arrival in the 11th century of Atisha, a renowned Indian master.

The Guge Kingdom lasted for over 600 years until 1630, when it was overthrown by the neighbouring country of Ladakh. Shortly before, in 1625, the Portuguese Jesuit Antonio de Andrade arrived at Guge and, with the King's permission, built Tibet's first Christian church. He was followed by a second Christian mission; but the growing influence of this alien religion caused a backlash. Alarmed lamas at Tsaparang conspired with the Ladakhis, and the subsequent invasion brought to an end a glorious though little-known kingdom.

Over the centuries the many temples and monasteries fell into disrepair, though they were protected by local residents. The fury of China's Cultural Revolution in the 1960s reached to even this remote quarter and invaluable works of art and architecture were destroyed. Even so, the remnants of Guge at Toling and Tsaparang still rank among the most important artistic monuments in Tibet.

Ruins of Tsaparang, capital of the Guge Kingdom in arid western Tibet. The buildings to the right are known as the White Temple and the Red Temple. Their interior walls are covered with marvellous mandala paintings in primary colors.

*(Previous Pages)*
The ruins of Tsaparang from a distance, with the Red Temple at
the bottom right. Thousands of people lived here in the 10th and
11th centuries, and in 1625 Antonio de Andrade, a Portuguese
missionary, founded a Catholic church at Tsaparang.

*(Above)*
A mural inside the White Temple at Toling. During the Cultural
Revolution the temple's roof was destroyed, exposing the paintings
to rain and erosion. This damaged image shows Mahavairochana,
the Celestial Buddha.

*(Left)*
The ruins of Toling Temple, once the centre of Buddhist culture
in western Tibet. A man contemplates the space where a large
Buddha statue once rested.

(Left)
The broken arm of a Buddha statue in the White Temple at Toling. An offering of paper money has been placed by the arm.

(Above)
Buddha heads piled together in the White Temple at Tsaparang. Some Chinese forced Tibetans to destroy Buddha statues at gunpoint.

*(Left)*
A photograph of Avalokiteshvara in Tsaparang's White Temple, taken by Li Gotami in 1948. She was the last outsider to see remnants of the Guge Kingdom before the destruction of the Cultural Revolution.

*(Right)*
A damaged 15th-century statue of Avalokiteshvara. The chest has been smashed to remove the treasures stored inside.

Toling's stupa in the evening sun. During the 11th century, when Toling was the centre of Buddhism in western Tibet, more than 100 stupas dotted the area. Some villagers still circumambulate their crumbling remains.

Statues and remnants of Buddhas, bodhisattvas and deities left in Tsaparang's White Temple. Of the original 18 statues only five remain and these have been badly damaged.

Two stupas guard the corners of the Gyaser Palace at Toling Temple.

A weathered stupa at Toling. This desolate region stands at 3,700 metres (12,000 feet) and is known today as Tsanda, with a village, prefectural office and garrison.

Ruins and reconstruction at Ganden Monastery, once one of Tibet's largest religious centres with more than 100 temples and over 3,500 monks. It now serves as a testament to China's efforts to destroy Tibetan culture.

Many plundered statues and objets d'art were taken away to China in the early years of Chinese occupation of Tibet. The battered statues here escaped being melted down and were returned to Ganden in 1989.

Damaged statues of the Buddha and Tibetan deities at Ganden tell the sad and poignant story of religious suppression over the past decades.

*(Above)*
Mutilated statues of the Buddha and materials for their restoration lie in a corridor at Palkor Chode Monastery in Gyantse.

*(Right)*
A terrible jumble of pots, pans, objects of daily use, censers and religious articles, even musical instruments, fill a courtyard at Sera Monastery. All were returned from China in 1982.

# Shattered Land of the Buddha

In northern India inthe foothills of the Himalayas lies the small town of Dharamsala which has been the headquarters of the Tibetan government in exile since the 1960s. The Dalai Lama lives here when he is not travelling and it is fair to say that his presence is the main reason for the visits of so many Westerners and others to this picturesque hill station. The scenery is lovely and the thousands of Tibetans who have made this town their home give it a special atmosphere of friendliness and color.

During my four trips to Tibet I was largely engrossed in my photography, concentrating on the grand monasteries and temples, vast grasslands and nomadic way of life. Only slowly did I come to realize how deeply the Tibetans are devoted to the Dalai Lama, and how many people have entrusted their lives to this one person. Throughout the suffering and hardship of Chinese rule, His Holiness has been a pillar of strength and support. As the focus of their faith and hope, he has enabled his people to endure the worst.

Thirty-five years ago nearly 100,000 Tibetans fled to India with the Dalai Lama, and today the flow of refugees continues. Between 20 and 30 new arrivals come to Dharamsala each day, and many of them have harrowing stories to tell.

In the room of a nunnery that was previously a private house, Kelsang Pemo, a 29-year-old nun, calmly talked to me about her days of torment five years earlier. Just next door a young nun who recently escaped from Tibet lay in bed, exhausted and sick, unaccustomed to the Indian weather.

Kelsang, along with eight other nuns and two monks, held a demonstration while circling Lhasa's Jokhang Temple. The date was May 17, 1988. It did not appear in Japanese papers at the time, though the morning edition of the July 14 Asahi Newspaper carried a short article, which quoted a government spokesman as saying, "On the 17th and 24th of May, demonstrations were held, but since both were conducted by nuns the people were few. Since then Lhasa has been calm." It was a minor demonstration, yet the reaction to it and the consequences for the participants were terrible.

According to Kelsang, she and the others first went quietly around the Jokhang Temple three times, each circuit taking about 15 minutes. Finally, upon reaching the police station across from the temple, they shouted "Freedom for Tibet! Long Live the Dalai Lama!" As soon as they started shouting, policemen appeared on every rooftop and in an instant they opened fire with automatic weapons. Though the firing was meant to warn and disperse the gathering crowd, one of the monks was shot in the leg and collapsed. Immediately armed police charged the small group, kicking and beating them. Kelsang was hit with the end of a gun stock and fell down from the blow. All were quickly thrown into army trucks and taken away. The injured monk continued to shout slogans for Tibetan independence despite his untreated, bleeding wound; each time he spoke out the Chinese police fired warning shots, cursed him and beat him repeatedly.

The following day the tortures began. The police wanted to know who was behind the demonstration. When the nuns told the truth that they themselves had organized the protest, the authorities did not believe them, thinking that young nuns could not possibly be so motivated. The police beat them, kicked them and made dogs bite them. Electric cattle-prods were used on their bodies, and many of the nuns lost consciousness. Their cell filled with the stench of an overflowing pot that served as the toilet. Just thinking of the torture that would continue the next day made them so frightened they could not sleep. The Chinese ill-will became clearer with each passing day.

Meals were very poor and the nuns sometimes found dirt mixed with the food. They even discovered that steamed bread had been dipped in a toilet. One day they were given yellow pills, said to be a help for their wounds. Supper was denied that night and it turned out the pills were simply a further form of torture, a "medicine" that induced hunger.

After a month of constant brutality by two policemen, the number suddenly increased to five. The men removed Kelsang's clothes, held her down and then forced an electric prod into her vagina. Kelsang recalled, "For an instant I felt a terrible burning pain in my belly and I lost consciousness . . . Hunger and torture had robbed all of us of our strength and spirit. My facial features had changed completely and it seems the police considered my state of health quite dangerous. They decided to bring in two women doctors. These women asked me where the pain was and I answered that it hurt all over. In response they spat in my face, said that was the medicine I deserved, and left the cell laughing scornfully."

Kelsang was released two months later but the effects of torture left her unable to walk properly so she was admitted to a hospital. In the meantime, nuns from her nunnery held three demonstrations that brought about a severe retaliation. All were banished from their nunnery and robbed of the right to practise religion. During this entire ordeal, Kelsang felt she might be killed but never did she expect to be expelled from her nunnery, denied her life's calling. At this moment she and others decided to flee Tibet to go to Dharamsala where they could live a life of religious freedom.

This billboard in a Lhasa street says; 'If it was not for the Communist Party of China, there would be no new, socialist Tibet.'

This defiant monk went into a blazing police station to rescue a friend during demonstrations in October 1987. He later died in prison.

Tibetan monks walk the streets of Dharamsala in northern India. They are more carefree than their compatriots in Lhasa who must live under the watchful eye of the People's Liberation Army.

Kelsang and another nun found people willing to smuggle them in a truck to Mount Kailash in West Tibet. Once there they met, by prior arrangement, four other nuns and two monks, and with the help of two nomad guides they began to cross the high peaks of the Himalayas. To avoid the army they took steep byways, often losing the way, and sometimes went without food for two or three days. One great difficulty was crossing freezing, swift mountain streams; none of them knew how to swim. After two months the little party finally reached Kathmandu, Nepal's capital.

Once free, Kelsang declared that to lose her life would be a worthwhile sacrifice if it helped the world realize what the Chinese were doing in Tibet. Forcing the Dalai Lama into exile, destroying the Buddhist religion and carrying on the occupation of her country were intolerable acts. Her courage, non-violent opposition and testimony are ways of bringing about that realization.

Dopé Adi, aged 58, is a woman who spent 27 years in prison until her release in 1985. Two years later she escaped to Dharamsala. She came originally from Kham, the province of East Tibet known for its strong, handsome people and fierce opposition to the People's Liberation Army in the 1950s and 1960s. Her husband was killed by the Chinese and she was captured while spying for the Tibetan resistance.

Of 300 women prisoners, only four survived the cruel prison experience. For years, Dopé Adi suffered from hunger; only her unbreakable faith kept her alive. She kept a paper cutting in the shape of the Buddha and made a rosary from a thread of torn prison clothing by tying tiny knots as beads. In this way she could pray silently, and to speak her prayers she covered her mouth with a piece of cloth. Whenever found out by the guards, they beat and tormented her.

Dopé Adi remembers that once a Chinese showed her his fat arm, cursed her and then said, "Look at you! Compare your emaciated arm to mine! What has the Buddha given to you? Give up your Buddhism if you want to live." All the while this man was sitting on a thangka, a sacred icon painting that usually is mounted and hung on a wall. He used it as a seat cover.

One day during forced labour at a road construction site Dopé Adi felt that her heart would break. Before her she saw truckload after truckload filled with Buddha statues being taken away to China where they were to be melted down for use in industry. For many days she witnessed this sacrilege and silently wept; she thought the end had really come for Tibet.

In Tibet, high monks are called Rinpoche (precious one) and they are highly revered for their learning, wisdom and holiness. Adi was shocked and horrified by the Chinese who systematically persecuted and tormented the rinpoches. Cruel acts were performed against them as a kind of "ritual" to show the Tibetans that such men were worthless and powerless.

One day Adi and other prisoners were taken to an area where high monks were forced to hold hammers in their handcuffed hands while guns pointed at their heads. They were made to smash green caterpillars one by one on a block, an act repugnant and unthinkable for religious men who honoured and protected all life.

A monk was made to crawl about on his hands and knees with a straw bridle in his mouth, carrying a woman on his back. Later it became known that this woman had gone crazy and had started to drink her own urine and paint her face with her own excrement. Everyone saw this as retribution for ridiculing the monk.

Sometimes the Chinese urinated on meditating monks, even forced monks and nuns to copulate in public, thus humiliating them to an unspeakable degree. All this was done to break the spirit of the Tibetans, destroy the religion and force the people to accept communism. The Chinese showed no mercy.

Severe oppression started towards the end of the 1950s, long before the outbreak of the Cultural Revolution in 1966. While Tibet underwent such nightmares, the Dalai Lama, who escaped to India in 1959, continued to preserve the Buddhist faith and teachings. This proved to be an immeasurable support for the people of Tibet.

At the end of our talk, Kelsang said, "By escaping I am worried about the danger I have put my family in, but as long as Tibet is not free I do not think about going back, nor do I have a place to return to. When I think of the Chinese who have treated me so cruelly, I cannot help but feel very sad for them. In prison, when I could not sleep from the pain of torture, many times I thought of the terrible karma they would have to carry into their next lives. If I was reborn and became like one of them . . . the thought was very frightening."

Devotees in Dharamsala hold a religious service in the rain. It takes Tibetan refugees some time to acclimatize to the rain, humidity and heat of this Indian town.

Dopé Adi spent 27 years in prison. She sits with the patched sheet that she took with her during the escape from her Chinese jailers.

The nun on the extreme left is Kelsang Pemo. In prison she became so weak she thought she would die without ever getting to see the Dalai Lama.

# The Kalachakra Initiation

The Kalachakra Initiation is a long religious ceremony performed by the Dalai Lama from time to time. It enables a person with the proper preparation into the vows, rituals, and yogic practices of the Kalachakra Tantra, an Unexcelled Yoga Tantra (a system of spiritual technology) of great complexity and refinement. It can also be attended by the faithful in general, who receive a blessing from the ceremony. Tibetans believe that once you look with faith upon the colored sand mandala at the center of the ritual, you will eventually be reborn in Shambhala, a northern paradise on earth that brings about a golden age in the future. Thus many people believe that the Kalachakra has a positive influence on social harmony and world peace; the Dalai Lama has led the ceremony ever more frequently in an effort to help and protect the earth. Now it takes place approximately once a year.

In August 1992, in a small Himalayan town called Kalpa in the Indian state of Himachal Pradesh, the 14th Dalai Lama presented the Kalachakra Initiation for the 17th time. Nine of the previous teachings had taken place at different sites in India, four in the West, one in Outer Mongolia and two in Lhasa in the 1950s. The 1992 teachings were held with the specific hope that the prayers and energy of the thousands of people gathered for a unified purpose would save Tibet from the crisis it faces. The event lasted for seven days and was attended by well over 25,000 men, women and children. Some had risked their lives by trekking over the Himalayas from Tibet to hear the Dalai Lama speak.

The scriptures and rituals of the Kalachakra Yoga teachings were brought to Tibet from India in the 11th century. They were collected and coordinated by the master scholar Buton Rinpoche (1294-1364) and became important through the practice of Tsong Khapa (1357-1419), the great philosopher and reformer, who founded the Gelugpa, or Yellow Hat Order of Tibetan Buddhism. All the Dalai Lamas have belonged to the Gelugpa Order, and the practice of the Kalachakra has been transmitted from master to disciple in an unbroken chain right up to the present Dalai Lama.

In religious terms, receiving the initiation is necessary to begin the cognitive and contemplative practices aimed at achieving a high state of spiritual realization. The ultimate goal is to become one with the Kalachakra ("Wheel of Time") Buddha, and thus accelerate one's own actual Buddhahood in the shortest possible time. The spiritual technology of the Wheel of Time is believed to enable the adept to accelerate mental and physical evolution in order to achieve the high state of absolute bliss, integrated within full mastery of the processes of death and reincarnation. Within Tibetan Buddhism the Kalachakra Initiation is said to be the most extensive and profound teaching and technology, and thereby affords us the best opportunity to make spiritual progress. Having a sincere heart, a good motivation, and a profound insight into the reality of the self are the best preparations for a devotee.

The initiation itself is highly complex. Before the formal commencement there are a number of preparatory ceremonies, such as the Disciple Ritual, the Ritual of the Site, and the Construction of the Mandala, all of which are essential for the events to come. These take several days to complete. The initiation proper is divided into 11 stages that culminate in the higher empowerments of the Perfection Stage which open up the advanced practices that lead to Buddhahood. The hourly and daily practices led by the Dalai Lama are precise and extremely detailed and frequently involve complex visualizations that assist in releasing the spiritual potential within each person.

In the Kalachakra, the symbolic relationship and unity between the cosmos and the human body is considered of the greatest importance. For example, the initiates are often asked to form a mental image of various deities and to merge with them in order to absorb their powers and to know first-hand the cosmic forces and attributes that the deities represent. In these contemplations, the energy released and the spiritual progress attained are believed to have the power to purify both the external, physical world and the internal, psychic world of each participant simultaneously. This is where the true value of the ceremony lies.

Whether they fully understood the theology and arcane vocabulary or not, Tibetans who attended the Kalachakra Initiation in Kalpa had a wonderful, joyous time. Simply by being there they shared in a profound event that benefitted everybody, and seeing the Dalai Lama day after day and hearing his words uplifted every open heart.

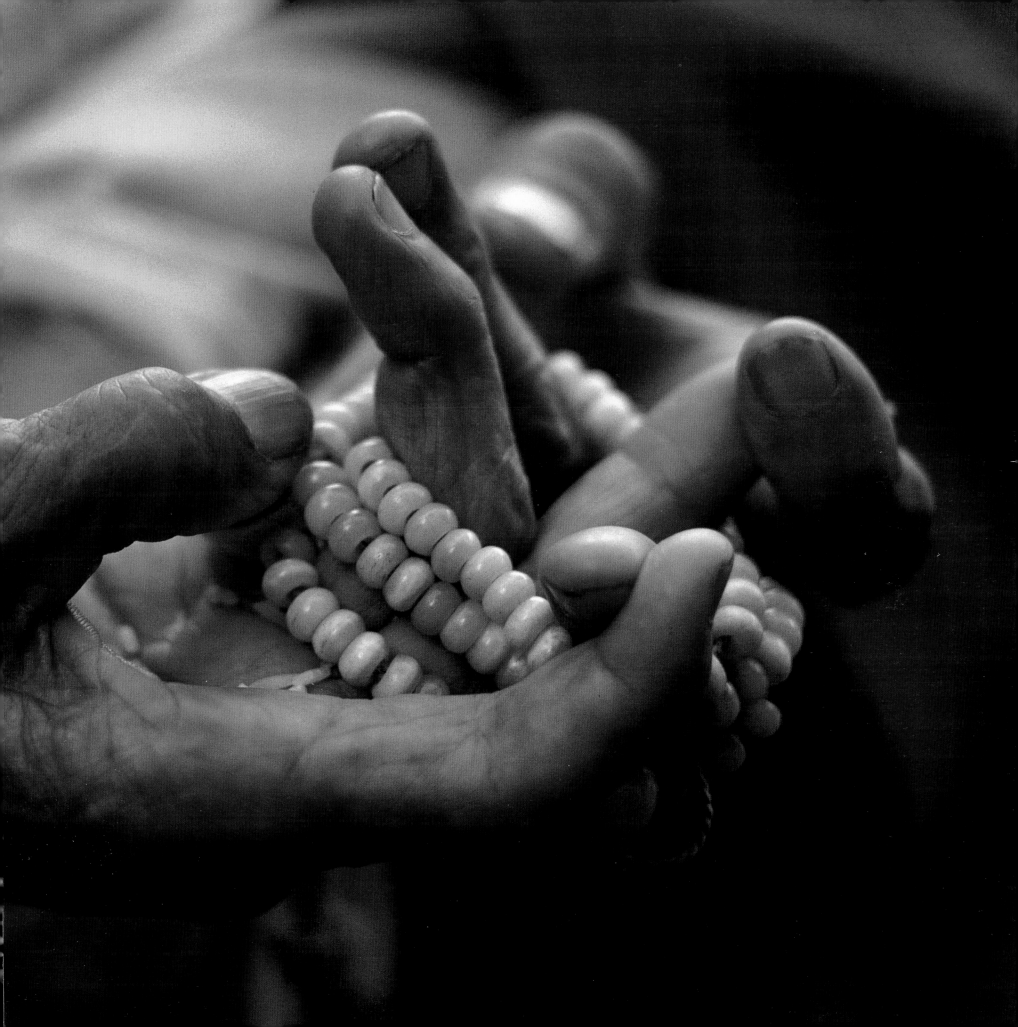

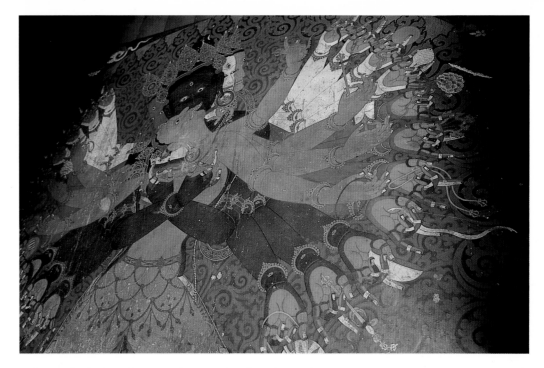

The Kalachakra deity embraces the female Buddha Vishvamata in a wall painting at the Great Stupa of Gyantse. During the Kalachakra Initiation a similar thang-ka is unfurled and the Dalai Lama symbolically becomes one with the deity to offer the initiation.

*(Prerious page)*
Fingers entwined with a rosary make the Mandala Offering, an act performed before and after prayer. The two raised fingers in the centre symbolize both the core of the mandala and Mount Sumeru, mythic centre of the Buddhist universe. The four finger-triangles symbolize the four continents of the world.

*(Left)*
His Holiness the Dalai Lama conducts the Kalachakra Initiation in front of 25,000 followers. The four-day ceremony is meant to bring wisdom, compassion, tolerance and peace to the world.

Recently arrived refugees in the courtyard of the Dalai Lama's Dharamsala residence are deeply moved after an audience with him.

*(Above)*
A nomad wears an image of the
Dalai Lama.

*(Right)*
A refugee family has just escaped
across the Himalayas and registered
at the Refugee Centre in
Dharamsala. Upon arrival they are
given a month's living expenses.

*(Left)*
A Kalachakra sand mandala nears
completion. As a sacred construction, the mandala becomes a celestial palace and the Kalachakra
Buddha-deity is invited to take up
residence in its centre. The Dalai
Lama merges with the deity to
properly perform the initiation.
When the initiation ends the mandala is destroyed and the sand is
thrown into a river.

*(Above)*
His Holiness the Dalai Lama draws
the first line of the sand mandala.
Sand from powdered marble in five
different colors is used. A slender
cone filled with sand and another
empty one are rubbed together to
create a vibration that allows a
small, controlled amount of sand to
emerge.

Thousands of devotees pray with the Dalai Lama; most are Tibetan refugees living in India.

*(Above)*
Indian villagers watch the Dalai Lama depart after finishing his teaching. Many local people are of Tibetan stock but have adopted Hinduism; one of the reasons for holding the Kalachakra Initiation here is to uphold Buddhism.

*(Right)*
'In the present world, we are faced with the unstoppable forces of science and scientific progress. To retain our humanity the role of religion and spirituality must become ever more important.'—The Dalai Lama.

# Interview with the Dalai Lama

To me, Dalai Lama is a title that signifies the office I hold. I myself am just a human being, and incidentally a Tibetan who chooses to be a Buddhist monk.

Freedom In Exile: Autobiography of His Holiness the 14th Dalai Lama

This is the Dalai Lama's view of himself. To Tibetans, however, the Dalai Lama is the incarnation of Avalokiteshvara, the Bodhisattva of Compassion, who has come to save mankind.

The 14th Dalai Lama was born in 1935 into a farming family in Amdo, northeastern Tibet, an area presently in Qinghai Province. He was recognized as the reincarnation of the 13th Dalai Lama by a search party that had followed a series of signs to his family's home. They took him and his relatives to the Potala Palace in Lhasa where, at the age of four, he was enthroned.

For centuries, Tibet was largely cut off from the rest of the world by its geography and an official policy of isolation. In 1950 this situation was threatened by the military might of Communist China. It was in that year that the Dalai Lama, aged 15, was invested with the political responsibility for Tibet. In 1951, China's People's Liberation Army reached Lhasa "to liberate the people from feudalism". On 10th March 1959, the residents of Lhasa rose up against the Chinese military occupation of Tibet. The Dalai Lama, whose life was in danger, escaped under the cover of night to India. There, at Dharamsala, he established the present Tibetan Government in exile.

There is an opinion that 'good, ancient' China has been destroyed and replaced by a 'bad' China, the product of communism, that has stemmed from a malign, Sino-centric view of the world. I would like to ask you for an impression of China from the Tibetan point of view.

Dalai Lama: I don't agree at all that China can be differentiated in that way. The Communist Party destroyed the feudal system and liberated the masses. It was later, under communist rule, that the people lost their spirit. It is true that a prosperous and a carefree China existed before the communist revolution of 1949, but it was only in cities near the sea, like Shanghai and Tientsin. People in the interior led impoverished lives under the Nationalist Party.

Generally speaking this may be so, but as a Tibetan whose country has, under the name of liberation, been ruined, what do you think?

Dalai Lama: Since the beginning of history the relationship between Tibet and China has been a repetition of disputes involving territory. We were never in a position to look at 'good' China objectively. However, before China became communist we shared a mutual recognition for each other based on a religious understanding. When I was a little boy my mother told me about an incident that I cannot forget. Many years ago when repeated famines struck neighbouring China many poor Chinese people came into Tibet. One day a couple holding their dead child in their arms came to our house begging for food. My mother, full of pity for the couple, gave them food and, pointing at their dead child, offered to help them bury it. But the couple shook their heads and said that they were going to eat the child. My mother was so surprised that she gave them all the food in the house. This is also a side of China that Tibet saw before the revolution.

*Did your Holiness feel solidarity with the student protesters in Tiananmen Square?*

Dalai Lama: Of course. Their protest was for human rights in China. It was basically different from the Tibetan movement. We are demanding our independence, ours is a dispute involving two different nationalities. The students were very much aware of the human rights violations that have been taking place in Tibet. After Tiananmen many Chinese have started showing interest in the Tibetan problem.

*Is that so? Among the Chinese that I have spoken to, including young intellectuals, I have been acutely aware of their Sino-centric worldview and their prejudiced attitude towards China's minorities. I cannot imagine them actively supporting the Tibetan independence movement . . .*

Dalai Lama: On the surface maybe. If they have a Sino-centric view that is because the only information they get about the outside world is controlled by the Communist Party.

*think many of the countries around China fear being swamped by the Chinese. Is this the case with Tibet?*

Dalai Lama: This is a very serious problem for Tibet and it requires an urgent solution. I discussed this when I met the Malaysian Prime Minister. Tibet does not have the means to prevent the influx that other independent and sovereign Asian countries have. Since 1983 the Chinese government has had a policy of encouraging immigration from China to Tibet, and according to our calculations, the Chinese population has now reached 7.5 million, thereby exceeding the Tibetan population of 6 million. We have been reduced to a minority in our own country.

*In the 40 years of Chinese occupation, what is the most important thing that Tibet has lost?*

Dalai Lama: It is the lives of more than one million Tibetans, many of whom died from starvation. This is something unheard of prior to the Chinese occupation. Further, nearly all of our 6,200 monasteries have been destroyed, along with a large number of statues of the Buddha. Gold, silver and precious stones accumulated over the generations have been plundered by the Chinese. And the tender, Buddhist hearts of the Tibetans have been trampled so badly . . .

*When I came to Dharamsala I heard that there is a difference between the Tibetans who have recently arrived from Tibet and the Tibetans who came earlier.*

Dalai Lama: That is right. The Tibetan refugees who came earlier were on the whole very gentle people, but the young Tibetans who have recently escaped from Tibet are very short tempered and they start fighting easily. Five months ago at their refugee camp in Bir (north India), they split up into two groups and started fighting. I reprimanded them and told them that 'if you like fighting so much go back to Tibet and fight the Chinese!' This is the result of violent Chinese oppression. People are suffering greatly, especially those who have escaped after being tortured in prison. Their character has often completely changed.

The four-year-old 14th Dalai Lama poses with the search party from Lhasa that found him, along with some local Amdo officials. The year is 1939. The Chinese photo caption incorrectly identifies him as five years old.

The Dalai Lama shakes hands with Mao Tsetung during his visit in Peking in 1954.

The Dalai Lama's party escapes to India in 1959. His Holiness is at center disguised in dark clothes. The Chinese reported that rebels compelled the Dalai Lama to flee.

*Your Holiness has said that in the next five to ten years there will be a big change in China. Could you explain what you think will happen?*

Dalai Lama: There is no need to say that when the senior politicians die, the freedom of political awareness cannot remain suppressed. The change may be sudden, like in the Soviet Union and Eastern Europe, or gradual, depending on the efficiency of the political process. For China I pray for a gradual change, otherwise I am afraid many lives will be lost.

*What do Tibetans think of the Dalai Lama today?*

Dalai Lama: Ha! Ha! Ha! (sudden laughter). When I visited the refugee camp in Mysore (south India), one of the refugees on seeing me shouted 'the Dalai Lama is walking in!'. His surprised tone suggested that he thought of me as a statue of Buddha or a thangka in a temple to be worshipped. Ha! Ha! Ha! . . .

*Travelling in Tibet I gained the impression that the Tibetan people's faith in your Holiness was their strength. I sometimes wonder what the consequences of something happening to your Holiness would be . . .*

Dalai Lama: (a long silence) If something was to suddenly happen to me, if I was to die for example, then Tibet could fall into chaos. The country could split into factions or there could be a serious clash with China. That is why we have been working to establish a government that can rule without the Dalai Lama. Last year (1992) we held elections in the exiled Tibetan community to inaugurate a new parliament and we are in the process of establishing the basis for a transfer of political power.

*In the near future do you think that you will have a chance to visit Tibet?*

Dalai Lama: As long as the Chinese side continues with its stubborn attitude I do not think so. Last year I made a proposal to the Chinese. I suggested that I could visit Tibet and pray with the people and explain and advocate non-violence. I am willing to go to Tibet at any time to soothe people's hearts and help them avoid ruin. My advocating non-violence would also benefit the Chinese. However, they did not even consider my proposal.

During the nine years I was in Tibet under Chinese occupation, whilst I was still a young boy, the Chinese would pull my ears as if they were chiding a naughty boy like this (gesturing with his right hand and laughing loudly). They would tell me when to wave to the public and what to say. It was the limit. If the Chinese still think that I can be treated like a toy then they are making a big mistake.

(The Tibetan interpreter could not directly translate that the Chinese treated the Dalai Lama as a toy and pulled his ears. Even though it was a joke, to the Tibetans even thinking about such a thing is disrespectful.)

*Was Mao Tse-tung the person who pulled your ears the hardest?*

Dalai Lama: No. The way I was treated by the leaders of the different provinces of China was worse. (At age 19 the Dalai Lama visited Peking and other parts of China.) However Mao Tse-tung must have been the one to give the orders.

*For your Holiness the most shocking thing must have been when Mao Tse-tung said to your face that 'religion is a drug'.*

Dalai Lama: Yes. When I realized that Mao, who had given me some useful advice, was nothing more than a destroyer of religion, I was extremely confused. He said that religion brought about two social evils; it hampered material and technological progress and caused the population to decrease, due to the celibacy of monks and nuns. Certainly, there was some truth in his words. I could have forgiven him if he had some understanding of religion. I think it is true that religion, if not practised properly, can be a drug. But Mao didn't seem to have made any attempt to understand religion. Communists have always looked at religion only from the materialistic point of view. Even today if there is any trouble in Tibet they blame it on religion. Tibetans are being robbed of the chance to practice religion correctly and are thus being driven away from it.

*The Chinese have always promoted the Panchen Lama and attempted to establish him as a rival to your Holiness. What is your opinion of the Panchen Lama?*

Dalai Lama: He always gave me encouragement. It is thought that he accepted the Chinese claim that Tibet is an inseparable part of China, but in his heart he did not. Until he passed away (in 1989, at the age of 52) under the most difficult circumstances, he did his best for Tibet and I am very grateful.

*Successive Indian governments have stated that they regard Tibet as a part of China. Have you protested about this?*

Dalai Lama: It is a typical political position; it is politics. It is enough to look at their unchanging kindness to exiled Tibetans to see that they don't believe it.

*The Chinese view of Tibet must have changed as a result of the develop-*

*ments in the communist bloc countries. Do you think the course of negotiations with them will also change?*

Dalai Lama: Whatever happens, non-violence is my policy. I have always emphasized that Tibet has been historically and culturally independent. However, approaching the issue of independence directly with the Chinese is impossible. So my priority is the happiness of the Tibetan people. Regarding Tibet's future, I have become much more optimistic. It is obvious that the world is becoming a place where justice prevails.

*What is the secret of your popularity with Westerners?*

Dalai Lama: I don't know. Maybe they think that the Dalai Lama represents the exoticism of Tibet and the Himalayas (laughter). Many of them think seriously about the Tibetan issue and are really interested in practicing Tibetan Buddhism. The majority believe that the Dalai Lama is a virtuous man, but they do not know the real me. Now, according to the Chinese, to them I am an anti-revolutionary and a parasite. Ha! Ha! Ha!

*In Japan, and in the West, there is a growing interest in new religions, especially among the young. How do you account for this?*

Dalai Lama: When a society encourages competitiveness and desire for material wealth, it also creates jealousy and even hatred of others. I think it creates an emptiness in people's hearts and leads them to religion. But what I always say is that what counts is not whether you believe in religion but whether you have compassion for others.

*When did your Holiness first realize that you were the reincarnation of the 13th Dalai Lama?*

Dalai Lama: I have never become aware that I am the reincarnation of the 13th Dalai Lama.

*Do you then remember any of the tests conducted by the search party that confirmed that you were the reincarnation of the 13th Dalai Lama?*

Dalai Lama: I don't remember anything about that time because I was very young. But I do remember that I was very happy to receive the blessings from so many people when I was recognized as the 14th Dalai Lama. And since then I have never felt any unhappiness about being the 14th Dalai Lama. My Buddhist beliefs make me feel deeply connected spiritually to the thirteen previous Dalai Lamas and to the Buddha himself. Will there be a fifteenth Dalai Lama? That is for the Tibetan people to decide. However, I will not be reborn under Chinese rule so that they can use me as a tool to rule Tibet. That much I know.

The Potala Palace of Lhasa.

In 1950, aged 15, the Dalai Lama took over the leadership of his country when Tibet was faced with the crisis of China's invasion.

The study and meditation seat of the 14th Dalai Lama in the Potala's White Palace. Behind this wall is His Holiness' bedroom, vacant since 1959.

# Modern Tibet

As with other great civilizations of the world, Tibetan culture developed around a major river, in this case the Yarlung Tsangpo which flows from west to east for 2,000 kilometres before cutting dramatically through the Himalayas to Assam, where it is known as the Brahmaputra.

Tibet's recorded history starts with King Nyatri Tsenpo (enthroned ca. 127 BCE). With the reign of King Songtsen Gampo (ca. 617–698), the might and influence of Tibet spread to many regions of West and Central Asia, and Buddhism was brought into the country. Over the centuries a unique culture emerged on the Roof of the World; reinforced by geographical isolation, a profound and valuable way of life developed.

Today the people of the Tibetan Plateau are facing a crisis. To understand the problem it is necessary to look at history and to learn about Tibet during the years between 1950 and the early 1980s.

Much of what we know about Tibet comes to us through the accounts of explorers, travellers, pilgrims, diplomats and spies. We have few accounts written by Tibetans themselves. The travellers' memoirs are unique records, full of extraordinary experiences and observations, but very few describe Tibet after 1950.

Following the Chinese occupation in 1950, Tibet's land, people and culture all but vanished from sight. Tibet was erased from the atlases of the world. In 1959 this situation altered briefly when the Dalai Lama first escaped into exile in India. The world's attention focused for a short while on Tibet, but soon the country disappeared once again into nearly two decades of darkness. These blank years were the result of international indifference to the plight of Tibetans under Chinese rule, and because China treated "liberated" Tibet as a closed region of the People's Republic of China.

In 1981, international concern and opinion finally induced China to stop hiding Tibet from the outside world and open it to limited tourism. Despite hardships and high costs, tourists continue to go to Lhasa, where they can see life on the high plateau and visit the few restored sites. These include the most prominent of the many historically important buildings, monasteries, temples, monuments and cultural artifacts that were destroyed or damaged in the 1950s or during the Cultural Revolution.

A result of tourism since 1981 has been that foreigners visiting Tibet have started to learn about the past 30 years and the disasters that befell the Tibetans. This knowledge has come largely from the mouths of common people. This new openness has not gone unnoticed by the Chinese, and the police and army continue to carry out atrocities and a policy of suppression. In the autumn of 1987 many foreigners witnessed anti-Chinese demonstrations in Lhasa and the subsequent crackdown. Since that time international opinion has intensified.

This scrutiny has been led by journalists, tourists, various governments, even by a group of non-partisan British parliamentarians. A report by the International Committee of Lawyers criticised the poor human rights record in Tibet. In fact, the situation in Tibet has been, and continues to be, nothing short of deplorable. Suppression, discrimination, torture, execution, forced labour, forced abortion—all of these human rights violations have been carried out and justified by the Chinese. By invoking specific socialist terms—especially "serf," "liberation," "interference in internal affairs," "splittist," "separatist," "imperialist," "traitor," "reactionary"—the Chinese have camouflaged their true intentions, causing the loss of 1.2 million Tibetan lives and the destruction of invaluable archives, scriptures and cultural treasures. The complete suppression of religion for 20 years and the near-obliteration of a civilization are indescribably terrible acts.

Foreign historians and contemporary Chinese historians differ widely on the interpretation of modern Tibetan history. Several facts stand out clearly, however: Before 1950, there were no Chinese settlers in Tibet; in 1950 the Peoples' Liberation Army invaded Tibet and crushed the small Tibetan Defense Force; in May 1951, Tibet was made a part of the People's Republic of China and abdicated its freedom to China by signing the "17 Point Agreement that includes the peaceful Liberation of Tibet"; and today there are nearly eight million Chinese settlers occupying the best land in Tibet, with the six million Tibetans driven into poverty in the marginal areas of the country.

In 1950, a year after the founding of the People's Republic of China, a Tibetan government delegation headed by Thupten Gyalpo went to India to reassert the sovereignty and independence of Tibet and to seek explanations from the Chinese ambassador in Delhi regarding a declaration made by Peking the previous year. In that declaration the Chinese stated that "Tibet is a part of China and the People's

Liberation Army is going to liberate the Tibetans from foreign imperialists". Talks with the ambassador achieved nothing, and furthermore the Chinese told the Tibetan side that China would take charge of Tibet's national defence and that it considered Tibet a part of China.

In October 1950, the Chinese army invaded eastern Tibet at the very moment that talks were being held. Not much time was needed for China, a populous, militarized country, to conquer Tibet, a Buddhist monastic state whose political institutions reflected religious priorities and allowed for only the most minimal military forces. Tibet had no choice but to accept the 17 Point Agreement, based on the fallacious premise that "Tibet is a part of China".

Nearly all foreign historians now consider China's intervention in 1950–51 as the armed invasion of Tibet. The Chinese claim that "Tibet is historically an inseparable part of Chinese territory" goes back over 700 years to the Pan-Asian Mongol Empire that conquered China and founded the Yuan Dynasty. This claim needs to be looked at carefully.

In 1244 Mongolia, having already conquered North and Central Asia, defeated the Sung Dynasty and established the Yuan dynasty in China. The Chinese side claims that in 1240, before Mongolia had established its rule, the invasion of Central Tibet by Prince Godan, son of Ogotai Khan, commenced relations with Tibet and set the precedent of Chinese sovereignty over Tibet. This, they claim, has stood from Mongol times down to the present day. We should consider how the world's map would change if China should be the owner of every country conquered by the Mongols, whose empire included Korea, Vietnam, Russia and the Middle East!

In 1913, a year after the Qing Dynasty's demise and in the context of the emerging modern nation-state system, the 13th Dalai Lama declared Tibet's formal independence. He had become aware of nationalism and world affairs; before this time a close historical relationship did exist between Tibet and China, but certainly not full suzerainty of one over the other.

Tibet shared a special type of "spiritual" relationship with the Mongol Dynasty and its successors based on mutual respect, cooperation and understanding of Buddhism. Today this is generally known as the "Priest-Patron" or "Patron-Lama" relationship. This institution began in 1244 when the great Buddhist scholar Kunga Gyaltsen, better known as Sakya Pandita, and his nephew Phagpa visited Prince Godan in Mongolia. This journey was undertaken to placate the Mongols and prevent them from launching an invasion of Tibet. Subsequently, Godan Khan assured the Tibetans that Mongols and Tibetans should be considered friends, with the Tibetans given spiritual authority over the Mongols. Later, in 1253, Phagpa became the spiritual teacher of Kublai Khan and his Sakya Order was given administrative power over Tibet within the international network of the Mongol Empire.

The evolution of this special relationship between the Tibetans and the Mongols is spelled out clearly in an extract from Tibet: A Political History, authored by the 20th-century Tibetan scholar Shakabpa.

"There was a definite change in the relationship between the Mongol ruler and the Tibetan Lama during Kublai's reign. A comparison of Godan's letter to Sakya Pandita with that of Kublai to Phagpa will reveal that the first is an example of correspondence from lord to subject, while the second is one of presentation from patron to lama. The latter is an example of the unique Central Asian concept of the Patron-Lama relationship, in which the temporal, lay power is given in return for the spiritual support of the religious power. This relationship between the Mongol rulers and Tibetan lamas cannot be defined in Western political terms. An insight into the attitudes of the Khan is shown by the lengths to which he went to please Phagpa, whom he acknowledged and supported both as his spiritual teacher and as the supreme authority in Tibet. This was maintained as the basis of a political-religious relationship between the Tibetans and the Mongols, and, in later times, between the Manchu emperors and the Dalai Lama."

For Tibet, the 300 years between the Mongols' departure from China (1368) and the Manchu conquest of China in 1644 was a period of rivalry among powerful nobles who relied on the support of different religious groups. Three Tibetan dynasties ruled the land, the Pagmodru (1349-1435), the Rinpung (1435-1566), and the Tsangpa (1566-1642). In 1642, the Great Fifth Dalai Lama was crowned as ruler of Tibet, beginning the Ganden Podrang monastic government that lasted until 1959 in Tibet and continues now in exile. During the Fifth Dalai Lama's 1652 visit to the newly established Manchu Qing Dynasty (1644–1911), the Patron-Lama relationship was re-established with the Manchu Emperors. Subsequently, the Manchu "Patrons" bestowed titles of spiritual honor on the "Lamas" to indicate their support of the monastic rulers, since the Manchu Emperors did not have actual rule over Tibet. The "Patron-Lama" relationship may be said to be the monastic government's strategy for national security, employing a foreign patron in order to avoid having to maintain any national military forces.

The Tibetan government invited the Manchus to intervene directly in its affairs a few times. In 1720 Manchu armies arrived to expel the Jungar Army, and twice, in 1788–91 and 1855–56, Manchu troops entered Tibet to repulse the Gurkha Army of Nepal. At these times the Manchus did protect the Dalai Lama and the Tibetan government, but used their temporary presence in Lhasa to establish permanently two ambassadors, known as Ambans. The Ambans represented the authority of the Manchu Qing Dynasty, and their presence was an excuse to demand recognition from the Tibetans.

After the fall of the Manchus, the 13th Dalai Lama expelled these foreign embassies and declared Tibet's full independence. Even though Tibet largely withdrew from the international scene between the years 1913–51, it absolutely conducted its own internal and external affairs and thus maintained its position as a completely independent country.

During this period Tibet attempted various social and administrative reforms, to bring it more in line with the status of a modern nation, but these proved to be largely unsuccessful. After World War II, many young people and some religious intellectuals were stimulated by the anti-colonial movement in India and the rise of communism in China. Their efforts to change Tibet were thwarted, however, and by the 1950s Tibet had been overtaken by its powerful neighbor.

Now, at the end of the 20th century, Tibet faces the real crisis of being overwhelmed by Chinese immigration. Already in Lhasa and other cities of Central Tibet, Chinese outnumber Tibetans and control nearly all shops and restaurants. In addition, the build-up of military bases continues in different parts of the country and this constitutes a major obstacle in the way of any reconciliation. As long as these military bases exist there seems to be no prospect for solving the crucial issues on the Roof of the World. At this time the "problem of Tibet" should definitely not be treated as an internal affair of China, but should receive increasing attention from the international community.

# Chronology of Tibetan History

*2nd Century BCE*
King Nyatri Tsenpo; founding of Yarlung Dynasty.

*7th Century CE*
King Songtsen Gampo; Buddhism introduced to Tibet; Jokhang Cathedral built.

*8th Century*
During King Trisong Detsen's reign, the empire reaches its greatest extent. Buddhism becomes the state religion; first monastery founded at Samye.

*9th Century*
King Lang Darma suppresses Buddhism, is assassinated and the dynasty collapses. Members of the royal family flee to western Tibet and later establish the Guge Kingdom.

*10th-11th Centuries*
Western Tibetan kings patronize the revival of Buddhism; the Indian Master Atisha (982-1054) visits Tibet in 1042, teaching for last twelve years of his life.

*1207*
Tibet sends a delegation to Genghis Khan. Good relations between Tibet and Mongolia.

*1239*
After Genghis Khan's death, eastern Tibet is invaded by Godan Khan's army, Sakya Pandita establishes friendly relations. A strong religious relationship is established between Tibet and Mongolia.

*1260*
Kublai Khan grants Phagpa Lama supreme authority over Tibet.

*13th–14th Centuries*
The Sakya Order rules Tibet, establishing precedent for the unique Tibetan invention of monastic government.

*1409*
Tsong Khapa (1357-1419) founds the Monlam Chenmo New Year Festival in Lhasa; Ganden Monastery develops as center of Tibetan Renaissance, sparked by founding of the reformed Gelugpa Order.

14th-17th Centuries
Pagmodruba, Rinpungpa, and Tsangpa secular dynasties rule Tibet.

*1447*
Gendun Drubpa (1391-1474, retrospectively known as the first Dalai Lama), a disciple of Tsong Khapa, founds Tashilhunpo Monastery.

*1642*
Gushri Khan rescues Gelugpa Order from persecution, defeats the armies of the Tsangpa King, and confers supreme authority on the Fifth Dalai Lama (1617-1682), who founds the Ganden Podrang monastic government, which still today survives in exile.

*1876*
Birth of the 13th Dalai Lama.

*1887*
Britain and the Manchu Qing Dynasty conclude a treaty regarding Burma and Tibet.

*ca. 1900*
The 13th Dalai Lama looks for support from Russia in order to check British and Chinese expansion.

*1904*
A British military expedition invades Tibet to pre-empt Russian involvement.

*1905–10*
China invades Tibet, conquers Kham Province, and sends an army to Lhasa to capture the 13th Dalai Lama.

*1910*
The 13th Dalai Lama takes refuge in India; China proclaims the Dalai Lama's dethronement.

*1911*
Fall of the Manchu dynasty; founding of the Republic of China.

*1912-13*
The 13th Dalai Lama expels remnants of Manchu army and reasserts Tibet's independence by issuing a proclamation in Lhasa.

*1914*
Tibet and Britain conclude the Simla Convention, settling the border between Tibet and India. The Chinese Government refuses to ratify the agreement, which then takes effect as a bilateral agreement between British and Tibetan governments.

*1933*
The 13th Dalai Lama dies.

*1935*
Birth of the 14th Dalai Lama.

*1940*
The 14th Dalai Lama is enthroned in the Potala Palace. Representatives from Britain, Nepal, Mongolia, Bhutan, Sikkim and China attend the ceremony.

*1942*
The Tibetan Government orders Nationalist China's Liaison Officer in Lhasa to leave the country.

*1945*
An English school is set up in Lhasa but soon closes because of opposition from the monastic establishment.

*1947*
Indian independence ends the British Tibet Policy.

*1949*
Founding of the People's Republic of China.

*1950*
The People's Liberation Army invades Kham; Tibet's army retreats. Tibet appeals to the United Nations and the Dalai Lama flees to the Sikkimese border.

*1951*
The 17-Point Agreement on the "peaceful liberation" of Tibet is signed under duress. The People's Liberation Army arrives in Lhasa; the food situation worsens because of large Chinese garrisons.

*1954*
India and China agree to the Five Principles for Peace. The Dalai Lama and Panchen Lama visit Beijing and attend meetings with Mao, Zhou, Deng, and other officials.

*1956*
In eastern Tibet (Amdo/Qinghai and Kham), Chinese cadres intensify anti-religious and "class struggle" activities, Chinese settlers take best lands in river valleys, and anti-Chinese guerrilla resistance spreads.

*1959*
The people of Lhasa rise up against the Chinese to prevent the seizure of the Dalai Lama; 100,000 Tibetans are killed by Chinese troops. China orders the dissolution of Tibet's government. The Dalai Lama escapes into exile in India, followed by 80,000 Tibetan refugees.

*1960*
Under the protection of the Indian Government, the Dalai Lama establishes the Tibetan Government in Exile in Dharamsala, India.

*1961*
A resolution supporting Tibet is adopted at the 16th General Assembly of the United Nations.

*1962*
Border war between India and China.

*1964*
The 10th Panchen Lama refuses to denounces the Dalai Lama, is tried and imprisoned. The Tibetan Autonomous Region is established.

*1966*
The Cultural Revolution begins in China.

*1976*
The death of Mao.

*1978*
The Panchen Lama released from prison.

*1979*
The first delegation representing the exiled Tibetan Government enters Tibet. Tibetans are allowed to visit relatives abroad.

*1980*
The second delegation representing the exiled Tibetan Government enters Tibet. China allows some religious freedom in Tibet.

*1983*
Systematic immigration of Chinese settlers into central Tibet.

*1985*
The fourth delegation representing the exiled Tibetan Government enters Tibet.

*1987*
The Dalai Lama proposes the Five-Point Peace Plan. Chinese denunciation sparks large demonstration in Lhasa; curfew imposed.

*1989*
Tiananmen Square massacre in China. The 10th Panchen Lama dies. Large demonstration in Lhasa. Martial law imposed and all foreigners expelled. The Dalai Lama wins the Nobel Peace Prize.

*1990*
Martial law in Lhasa lifted.

*1991*
Fortieth anniversary of the "peaceful liberation" of Tibet.

*1992*
The Tibetan Autonomous Region is designated a Special Economic Region.

*1993*
The Chinese Government rejects the Dalai Lama's One-country, Two-governments proposal. Systematic "population transfer" of Chinese settlers into central Tibet intensified.

*1995*
U.S. Congress passes resolution that Tibet is a nation under foreign occupation; Dalai Lama announces discovery of reincarnation of Panchen Lama, as boy from Nagchuka, Gendun Chokyi Nyima; China rejects Dalai Lama's choice, places boy and his family under arrest in China.

*1996*
Population of Lhasa reaches half a million, not counting military garrisons; Chinese outnumber Tibetans ten to one in all Tibetan cities. Poverty of marginalized Tibetans reaches new levels. Chinese install their own choice for Panchen Lama, start new campaign against Dalai Lama, provoking demonstrations, arrests, bloodshed. German, British, French parliaments condemn China's human rights violations in Tibet. Chinese policy hardens with new rulers intent on solidifying their power for transition after imminent death of Deng. Tibetan situation static.

*1997*
Death of Deng Xiaoping.

# Afterword

In the sections on Buddhism and the Guge Kingdom, I wrote about King Lang Darma, who destroyed the ancient kingdom of Tibet by persecuting Buddhism in the 9th century. Lang Darma's hatred for Buddhism was so intense that he closed all the temples and monasteries and forced the monks to give up the religious life. Any who disobeyed suffered death. He thus earned the hatred of the people and in 842 was assassinated.

Now, 1,150 years later, Tibetan Buddhist culture is once again facing the threat of extinction. China invaded Tibet in 1950 under the pretext of liberating it from "feudalism", the backwardness of Tibet being a problem that the Tibetans were working to solve in their own way. But once the Tibetans realized the true aim of the Chinese—to subjugate their country and impose communism—a rumour spread that Mao Tse-tung was the reincarnation of Lang Darma. In the Tibetan scheme of things this made sense, but there was a major problem. Unlike Lang Darma, whose reign perished due to the actions of a single monk-assassin, Mao Tse-tung was a not an opponent who could be easily opposed or toppled.

One irony in my life is that Mao Tse-tung led me to Tibet. I first encountered the Tibetan world when I was collecting material and writing about the Red Army's Long March of 1935. I had no knowledge of the Sino-Tibetan political problem but I became puzzled by the absence of temples and monasteries written about in the Long March histories. When the Red Army soldiers passed through Tibetan territory, they rested for days in various temples and monasteries, but when I visited these areas for my story, I could not find any of the buildings described. They were supposed to be large structures, able to house thousands of men. Only later did I discover that they had all been destroyed during the first few decades of the Chinese occupation.

Though I found no temples or monasteries, I did find carefully preserved Long March monuments. Among these were slogans written on wooden shutters by soldiers of the Red Army.

"Overthrow the evil military clique slaughtering the Muslims and the Tibetans!"

"Freedom of religion. Protect the monks."

"The Red Army will not kill the Muslims or Tibetans!"

At the time of the Long March the Red Army was on the run from Nationalist forces. The slogans reveal their desire not to antagonize any of Tibet's populations. Later, however, as the Red Army gained the upper hand and became the People's Liberation Army, Mao Tse-tung ordered his men to "liberate" all Tibet. Monks and laypeople who resisted were arrested or killed.

In the fateful year of 1935, not far from the very route taken by the Long March, something extremely fortunate happened. There occurred the birth of a boy said to be the incarnation of Avalokiteshvara, Bodhisattva of Compassion. This child would grow up to become the Dalai Lama and carry the weight of Tibet's tragedy on his shoulders.

Twenty-four years after the Long March, the 14th Dalai Lama escaped into exile in India in 1959. The country that had existed as a uniquely spiritual land for 1,400 years collapsed. Perhaps it is more correct to say that the Tibetans lost their country.

China has now abandoned communism for market socialism and is rapidly becoming a major power in Asia. The social forces that have accompanied this economic development are also threatening the fabric of society, and the enormous changes, good and bad, are engulfing the Tibetan Plateau as well. How will the Tibetan people respond to what is happening? How will Buddhism adapt and survive in the face of such challenges? And will the dream of independence for Tibet ever be realized?

# Acknowledgements

In the summer of 1988, from the vast grasslands of Ngaba in eastern Tibet, I started photographing and writing about Tibet. More than four years later, after visiting the Nagchu area north of Lhasa at the end of 1992, I finished. During this period I visited Tibet five times and also spent valuable weeks with Tibetan exiles in Dharamsala in northern India.

I would like to thank the many people whose devoted help allowed me to obtain difficult travel permits and make travel arrangements. Because of the nature of this book, I thought it wiser not to mention the names of Tibetans living in Tibet or the various Chinese who assisted me.

More than anyone else, I would like to express my gratitude to His Holiness the Dalai Lama. His Holiness granted me precious time for an interview and also wrote the foreword to this pictorial book. Even thirty years after losing their country, I believe there is no refugee community in the world so strongly bound together as that of the Tibetans. The reason for this is the immense faith the Tibetan people have placed in His Holiness, who is more than just a religious leader.

In Dharamsala I was helped by Tenzin Geyche Tehong, Tempa Tsering and Tsering Tashi in locating materials and arranging interviews.

Among the people who testified to the suffering and terror in Tibet, I would like to record the names of Kelsang Pemo, Dopé Adi and Jhampa Phuntsok. In making contact with the exiled government in Dharamsala I received assistance from Dawa N Lhupchung, Lhakpa Tsoko and the staff of the Liaison Office of His Holiness the Dalai Lama in Japan.

I would like to thank from my heart Mr Lungtok, who began as the interpreter for the interview with His Holiness and then also helped me write and check the photograph captions, and Deki T Tsoko, who undertook the task of translating all the text into English.

Many thanks also go to all the other people who helped me along the way. Among these, I would like to mention Minao Kitamura, the television director with whom I went to Mount Kailash, Ayako Sadakane, a Tibetologist, Kimiaki Tanaka, a Tibetan Buddhist scholar who journeyed with me to Tsaparang despite suffering from altitude sickness, and finally Shinichi Nakazawa an anthropologist of religion who has contributed to these pages.

I am much indebted to Pacific Press Service and The Guidebook Company for their close team work, which made the creation of this book possible. `